art / shop / eat
SAN FRANCISCO

Marlene Goldman
Christopher Springer
Richard Sterling
Tara Weaver

PACIFIC

SAN FRANCISCO

N

O C E A N

Golden Gate Bridge
Fort Point

Doyle Dr

101 US

1

PRESIDIO

Lincoln Park

SEACLIFF

LAKE

PRESID

HEIGH

Blvd

California

Euclid

Av

126

127

Arguello

Lobos   Av   Geary

Blvd

Presidio

Park

RICHMOND

25th

St

Fulton

Stanyan

Fulton

Great

OCEAN
BEACH

Golden   Gate

Park

Way

100

Hwy

Lincoln

7th

St

Judah

19th

Sunset

GOLDEN
GATE
HEIGHTS

SUNSET

1

FOREST

A note on maps. Commercial galleries, restaurants and shops are each
identified with a coloured, numbered dot in the text and on the chapter maps.
Some restaurants or shops that are close together may share a number to
conserve space.

Taraval

PARKSIDE

Av

WEST
PORTAL

Portola

Hwy

Blvd

ST. FRANCIS
WOOD

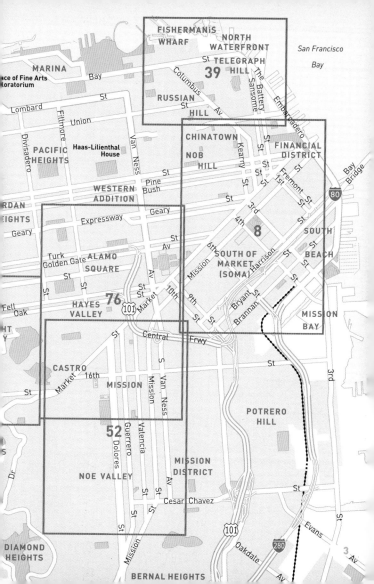

Downtown & SoMa

The Mission District

Hayes Valley & Civic Center

The Haight

Clement St. & the Richmond District

CONTENTS

introduction

San Francisco is sheer serendipity. Undulating hills, a shoreline on three sides, and California's most unusual cityscape collaborate to beguile visitors.

In this guidebook we've zoned the city around its five key museums. **Downtown & South of Market** features the contemporary works of the San Francisco Museum of Modern Art, while the **Mission District** highlights the colourful outdoor murals of this vibrant neighbourhood. **Hayes Valley & Civic Center** showcases the exquisite pieces of the Asian Art Museum, while the **Haight** covers the new De Young Museum. The fifth and final zone, **Clement St. & Richmond**, focuses on the tradition-steeped collection of the California Palace of the Legion of Honor.

A hundred years have passed since the temblor that shook this gorgeous city into rubble, but San Franciscans still live with the reality of earthquakes. For museum-goers, this has been a boon; lately, tectonic instability has done wonders for San Francisco's museum scene, with buildings that are bigger, better and safer—and architecturally more interesting.

But San Francisco is more than just a feast for the eyes. So once you emerge from the museum doors, follow our recommendations to some of the best food in the country—Mexican, Chinese and Italian are all famous here, but it's also possible to find almost anything else, from Peruvian to Afghan. We'll also direct you toward shopping of all kinds, whether your tastes run to discovering one-of-a-kind boutiques or riffling the pages in used bookstores. The sections in the back of the guide, **Entertainment** and **Planning**, give advice on arriving, finding accommodation and getting around, as well as where to drink and hear music, while the **Art Glossary** makes sure you know about what San Francisco has to offer.

We hope this guide helps you get to know San Francisco—and, more importantly, to love it.

DOWNTOWN & SOUTH OF MARKET

San Francisco Museum of Modern Art (SFMOMA)

OPEN	11 am–5.45 pm; Fri–Tue; 11 am–8.45 pm, Thur. In summer from 10 am. Closed Wednesday and holidays.
CHARGES	$10 adults, $7 seniors, $6 students (with ID). Extra for special exhibitions. Admission is half price Thursday evenings, free first Tuesday of each month.
GUIDED VISITS	Free tours; audio guides $3
DISABLED ACCESS	From main entrance, wheelchairs available
SERVICES	Museum shop, Caffè Museo, coat check on ground floor; store and café open at 10 am
TELEPHONE	(415) 357-4000
WEB	www.sfmoma.org
MAIN ENTRANCE	151 3rd St., between Mission and Howard Sts. Parking is available at the museum's garage off Minna St., just north of the museum.
GETTING THERE	BART or Muni to Montgomery Street Station; #30 Stockton bus to Howard Street

HIGHLIGHTS

Henri Matisse's *Femme au Chapeau*	2nd floor, Room 200
Constantin Brancusi's *La Négresse Blonde*	2nd floor, Room 201
Collection of works by Paul Klee from the Djerassi Art Trust	2nd floor, Room 202
Diego Rivera's *Flower Carriers*	2nd floor, Room 204
René Magritte's *Les Valeurs personnelles*	2nd floor, Room 205
Mark Rothko's *No. 14*	2nd floor, Room 206
Objects from the Architecture and Design Collection	2nd floor, Room 215
Photography Collection	3rd floor

When it opened in 1935, the San Francisco Museum of Art (the word 'modern' was only added to the name in 1975) was the only museum on the West Coast devoted solely to 20th-C art. It is known for its world-class photography collection as well as strong holdings in painting and sculpture, particularly in Abstract Expressionism. The museum has spent the past decade acquiring aggressively, and a recent shift in approach has led the museum to devote half of its 50,000 square feet of gallery space to selections from the permanent collection.

THE BUILDING

The SFMOMA building, designed by Swiss architect Mario Botta, has a stepped façade of brick and is crowned with a truncated cylinder of black and white granite, a distinctly geometrical Botta touch. The use of patterned textures is continued inside, where bands of polished and textured black stone alternate throughout the lobby. Botta—inspired by his time spent studying in Italy—designed an open, piazza-like lobby, ringed by the museum store, café, cloakroom and other service areas. On either side of the main staircase are large-scale works by Sol LeWitt; the colour makes an interesting contrast with the black and white of the interior. Natural light filters down through Botta's cylindrical tower and through the glass bridge that hangs in the atrium.

THE COLLECTION

From Botta's atrium, ascend the staircase or take the elevator to the second floor, where paintings and sculptures from the permanent collection are displayed in the collection **MATISSE AND BEYOND❶**.

SECOND FLOOR

The first gallery, *Room 200*, contains one of the museum's most famous paintings, **Matisse's** *Femme au Chapeau* (1905). The bright and discordant colours Matisse employed in this painting of his wife caused one reviewer to declare that it had been painted by wild beasts (*fauves*). This inspired the christening of a new art

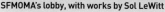
SFMOMA's lobby, with works by Sol LeWitt

movement, Fauvism, the name of which symbolises a departure from the accurate representation of figure and colour.

Also in this gallery are Matisse's paired portraits of *Sarah and Michael Stein* (1916). Michael Stein was Gertrude Stein's older brother, and he and his wife were great patrons of Matisse. They also introduced him to **Pablo Picasso**, thereby facilitating a relationship that had a profound impact on art. Also in this room is a landscape by **Andre Derain** and the final sketch by Matisse for *Le Bonheur de Vivre* (1905-1906), all of which show the Fauvists' expressive and untraditional use of colour.

A comparison of *Tête de Trois Quarts* (1907) by Picasso and *Violin and Candlestick* (1910) by **Georges Braque** shows each artist struggling to represent the essence of three-dimensional objects on a flat canvas. Their use of a technique of splintering and reconstructing the image to do so became known as Cubism.

Continuing on to *Room 201*, you'll find the characteristically ovoid *La Négresse Blonde* (1926) by **Constantin Brancusi**. The showpiece

SFMOMA

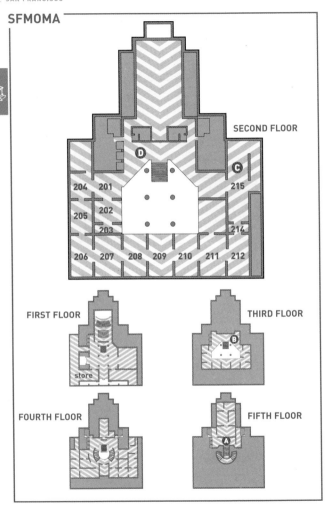

SECOND FLOOR

FIRST FLOOR

THIRD FLOOR

FOURTH FLOOR

FIFTH FLOOR

of the room, however, is **Marcel Duchamp**'s famous and infamous *Fountain*. The piece you see here is one of eight replicas commissioned by Duchamp in 1964 to replace the 1917 original, which was lost soon after it was displayed; in a strange reversal of the usual method of art reproduction, the replicas have been meticulously designed to reproduce the first readymade and are worth far more. The story of *Fountain* is legendary: Duchamp, known for his brilliant and subversive *Nude Descending a Staircase, No. 2*, submitted a urinal signed 'R. Mutt' to the Society of Independent Artists.

Also in this room are paintings by German painters **Max Beckmann** and **Franz March**, a founding member of the Blue Rider (*Der Blaue Reiter*) Group. On the right hand wall are works by Dutch artist **Piet Mondrian**. The second piece, *New York City 2* (1941), was unfinished when Mondrian died, but the pattern and placement of the coloured tape and pinholes provides insight into Mondrian's creative process.

At the far end of this room is the **PAUL KLEE STUDY CENTER** *(Room 203)*, where a rotating series of images from the Djerassi Art Trust illustrate the career of this Swiss-born painter and graphic artist.

Retracing your steps to the first gallery, turn left and enter *Room 204*. On the far right wall are works by the Mexican painters **Frida Kahlo** and her muralist husband **Diego Rivera**. The couple spent time in San Francisco in the early 1930s while Rivera worked on several mural commissions, and Kahlo gave this *Double Portrait* (1931) to her husband's patron, Albert Bender, to thank him for securing their visas. The neighbouring *Flower Carriers* (1935) by Rivera was a gift from Bender to the museum.

Paintings by **Georgia O'Keeffe** on the side wall of the gallery include *Lake George* (1922) and *Black Place I* (1944), which show the painter's fascination with the simplification of landscape and natural forms. On the far left side of this gallery look for Picasso's *Les Femmes d'Alger (Women of Algiers)* 1955 and *Enigmatic Combat* (1936-37) by Armenian artist **Ashile Gorky**, who was greatly influenced by Picasso's work. Also in this room look for works by **Joan Miró** and **Alexander Calder**, whose *Lone Yellow* mobile (1961) hanging overhead was inspired by Piet Mondrian's geometric paintings.

Room 205 has **Jackson Pollock**'s *Guardians of the Secret* (1943) on the right wall. At that time, Pollock had yet to develop the drip technique for which he became known, and was still working with abstract shapes. The influences on this work vary from Native American artistic traditions to the work of Picasso and Mexican muralist David Alfaro Siqueiros. Also in this room, look for work by the surrealist painter **Yves Tanguy** and *Les Valeurs personnelles* (1952) by **René Magritte**.

Room 206 is dwarfed by the monumental **Mark Rothko** painting, *No. 14* (1960), on the far wall, each colour contrasting with and intensifying the other to rouse the viewer's senses.

The next gallery, *Room 207*, is devoted to the work of **Clyfford Still**. A contemporary of Rothko, and also a 'colour field' painter, Still's work differs in that the colours are applied with a thick impasto and feature jagged edges, as if one colour was torn away to reveal another.

With the following gallery, *Room 208*, we transition from Abstract Expressionism into the Pop Art movement, which tried to erode the gulf between high and low art. **Jasper Johns**' *Lands End* (1963) is a good example of the kind of intended irony that characterised the Pop Art movement, with the names of colours stencilled onto the canvas in non-corresponding colours. Also in this room are works by **Andy Warhol** and **Claes Oldenburg**, and **Robert Rauschenberg**'s *Collection* (1954), with its bits of newspaper.

Rauschenberg's work continues in *Room 209*, where an untitled work of 1955 combines painting and sculpture by incorporating a torn shirt, a funnel, and a ball of string. Here you'll also find Jasper Johns' *Flag* (1958).

The following gallery, *Room 210*, features work by **Richard Diebenkorn**. His Ocean Park series (*Ocean Park 54*, of 1972, is displayed here) is an evocation of the light and space of the Southern California neighbourhood where he lived. There are also earlier, more figurative works here, such as *Cityscape I* (1963).

On the right hand wall of *Room 211* is **Frank Stella**'s *Zambezi* (1959), one of his early 'Black Paintings,' a black canvas with a pattern of unpainted stripes. A precursor of Minimalism, Stella moved away from representational images and towards art as a visual object. Also in this room is **Richard Artschwager**'s *Triptych III* (1967) of marbled Formica.

Room 212 is the final gallery in this series. On the right hand wall is **Louise Nevelson**'s monumental *Cascade* (1964). Nevelson created sculptures of found objects painted black, white, or gold, the single colour bringing out the shadows of the sculpture and emphasising the structural quality. Also in this room is **Donald Judd**'s ode to Minimalism, in an untitled work of 1973. The stainless steel series of identical boxlike figures affixed to the wall shows the geometric precision favoured by the movement, which focuses on the purity of form and the possibility of perfection.

The next room is a transition zone into **ART OF DESIGN** , selections from the museum's Architecture and Design Collection. While the selection here rotates on a regular basis, keep an eye out for works by **Frank Gehry** and **Walter Gropius**, and furniture by **Eames**. You may also see familiar objects, such as a Ducati Senna 916 Series III motorcycle (1997) and an Apple Titanium G4 Powerbook (2001). A walk-through passageway at the far end of this room features a themed graphics exhibition.

The remaining galleries on the second floor are used for special exhibitions. The museum's permanent collection continues with the photography exhibit on the third floor.

THIRD FLOOR

PICTURING MODERNITY features selections from the museum's collection of over 10,000 photographs. Though items rotate on a regular basis, in order to protect the photographs, the collection is laid out in a fairly chronological manner. Upon entering, turn immediately to your left, where you will see examples of daguerreotypes and early photographs. In 1839, **Louis-Jaques-Mandé Daguerre** developed the Daguerreotype process, by which a single reproduction of an image could be affixed to a silver-coated copper plate. Look also for early images by **Felix Nadar**, **George R. Fardon**'s pictures of San Francisco (1856), and work by **Eadweard Muybridge**,

Robert Rauschenberg *Port of Entry* (1998)

who is perhaps best known for his 1872 photographs of horses in mid-gallop done for Leland Stanford, then governor of California.

Continuing, you will see images by **Henri Cartier-Bresson**, **Alexander Rodchenko** and **László Moholy-Nagy**. In the second room you can follow the development of photography in America, where two centres of influence emerged. In New York, **Alfred Stieglitz** fought for recognition for the new art form, forming a group of photographers called the Photo-Secession, arranging gallery exhibitions and editing the magazine *Camera Work*. In 1923, Stieglitz was asked to submit photographs to the Museum of Fine Arts, Boston—the first photographer to be invited.

Here in San Francisco in the 1930s, a new style was emerging. The photographers **Ansel Adams**, **Imogen Cunningham**, **John Paul Edwards**, **Preston Holder**, **Consuelo Kanaga**, **Alma Lavenson**, **Sonya Noskowiak**, **Henry Swift**, **Willard Van Dyke**, **Brett Weston** and **Edward Weston** announced at the de Young Museum (see p. 101) that they had formed Group f/64. The group—named after an aperture—rejected Pictorialism in favour of a style of stripped-down photography. As Edward Weston phrased it, 'the camera should be used for a recording of life, for rendering the very substance and quintessence of the thing itself'.

Follow the side of this room around to see Depression-era works, representative of time in which photography became a driving force, documenting the country's shift from rural to industrial and influencing millions of people through the publication of photo magazines such as *Life*. **Dorothea Lange** and **Walker Evans** are among the best-known photographers hired by the Farm Security Administration to document and publicise the situation and the work of the FSA.

The third room follows the evolution of photography to the current day. From the street scenes of photographers such as **Leon Levinstein** to the portraits of American life by artists like **Robert Frank**, **Diane Arbus** and **Andrea Modica**, photography has continued to capture the development of American society. Keep an eye out for work by contemporary photographers such as **Nikki Lee**, whose 'projects' (such as the Skateboarder Project, the Hispanic Project and the Lesbian Project) involve integrating herself into a subculture before capturing it—and herself—on film.

The remaining sections of the third floor are devoted to special exhibits from the photography collection and visiting exhibits. The fourth floor of the museum also houses special exhibits (sometimes requiring a separate ticket). Continue to the fifth floor—go via the elevator if you are scared of heights, as taking the stairs requires a walk across a footbridge suspended high in the museum atrium.

FIFTH FLOOR

The fifth floor has been recently rededicated to selections from the permanent collection. The title **BETWEEN ART AND LIFE** ⓑ was inspired by a 1961 quote by Robert Rauschenberg: 'Painting relates to both art and life. Neither can be made. (I try to act in that gap between the two.)'. Housed in the tower topping Botta's design, the exhibition area features high ceilings and lends itself to large-scale installations, such as work by **Robert Gober**, **Kara Walker** and **Gordon Matta-Clark**. The exhibit opens with *Port of Entry* (1998), a monumental collage by Rauschenberg (see opposite).

George Herriman *Krazy Kat*

in the area

Cartoon Art Museum 655 Mission St., (415) 227-8666, www.cartoon
art.org. Open 11 am–5 pm, Tue–Sun; closed Mon. $6 general, $4
seniors and students, $2 children (6–12). The Cartoon Art
Museum was founded in 1984, when a group of local cartoon
enthusiasts pooled their own collections and began organising
exhibitions. In 1987, with a donation from *Peanuts* creator Charles
M. Schulz, the museum moved to a permanent location in the
SoMa district. The only American museum specialising in
cartoons, the collection now numbers 6,000 original pieces and
holds seven major exhibitions each year on top of an ongoing
exhibition on the history of cartoon art. Recent retrospectives
include the works of *Bizarro* creator Dan Piraro. Take BART or
Muni to Montgomery St. Station. **Map p. 8, 3B**

Yerba Buena Center for the Arts 701 Mission St., (415) 978-ARTS,
www.ybca.org. Open 12 pm–10 pm, Thur–Sat; 12 pm–5 pm, Sun,
Tue and Wed. $6/$3; free first Tues of the month. Across Third St.

from SFMOMA is the Yerba Buena Center for the Arts. Founded in 1993, Yerba Beuna is devoted to adventurous contemporary art. By providing residencies to artists in a variety of media—visual arts, performing arts and film/video—Yerba Buena offers a look at developing, multidisciplinary art by local and international artists. While there is no permanent collection, four gallery shows a year feature the work of artists-in-residence (there have been recent shows by Erwin Wurm, Jose Alvaro-Perdices and Yunhee Min). **Map p. 8, 3B**

San Francisco Museum of Craft+Design 550 Sutter St., (415) 773-0303, www.sfmcd.org. Open 10 am–5 pm, Tue–Sun; until 7 pm on Thur. $5/$3, free for children under 18. Opened in October of 2004, the San Francisco Museum of Craft+Design focuses on national, and international contemporary design. The museum is devoting its 3,500-square-foot space to themed exhibits; the inaugural exhibit, 'Dovetailing Art and Life', features furniture and objects from the collection of Sylvia and Gary Knox Bennett. The collection includes work by Wendell Castle, Judy Kensley McKie, Arthur Espenet Carpenter and Sam Maloof. Take the #4 Sutter bus to Stockton St. **Map p. 8, 1B**

The Contemporary Jewish Museum 121 Stuart St., (415) 344-8800, www. jmsf.org. Open 12 pm–6 pm, Sun–Thur. $5/$4. Founded in 1984, the Contemporary Jewish Museum (formerly the Jewish Museum of San Francisco) explores the history and art of the Jewish experience and Jewish expression. A venue for art, music, film, literature and debate, recent exhibits include work by conceptual artist Sophie Calle and themed exhibits featuring the work of Bruce Nauman, Gerhard Richter and Ed Ruscha. The museum's location is temporary; Daniel Libeskind is transforming the historic Jessie St. Substation, designed in 1907 by Willis Polk, into a permanent facility. Take BART or Muni to Embarcadero Station. **Map p. 8, 4A**

Alcatraz www.nps.gov/alcatraz. You can explore the island, America's most legendary prison, on your own ($11.50 for adults) or with an audio narration ($16 for adults). Call (415) 705-5555 for reservations (recommended, particularly during tourist season). This maximum-security island penitentiary opened in 1934 to

Coit Tower

isolate the nation's most hardened criminals; guests have included Al Capone and 'Machine Gun' Kelly. Although close to the peninsula of San Francisco, the Rock is surrounded by swirling, chill waters. Still, some inmates risked everything to escape, and two actually made it to the mainland before being apprehended (five more were never discovered and are presumed drowned). The prison closed in 1963, mainly because of the excessive cost of running an island prison, but Alcatraz's drama was not over: an occupation of the island in 1969 by Native American activists lasted a year and a half. Alcatraz can be reached by ferry from Pier 41 on Fisherman's Wharf. **Map p. 39, 2A**

California Academy of Sciences 875 Howard St. (between 4th and 5th Sts.), www.calacademy.org. Open 10 am–5 pm daily. $7 regular admission/$4.50 for ages 12–17 and seniors/$2 for ages 4–11. Free on the first Wednesday of each month. A long-time fixture of Golden Gate Park (see p. 111), this premier science and natural history museum—with its webbed, finned and four-legged residents—has been relocated to temporary quarters in the SoMa district. In 2008 the Academy is scheduled to return to the park and a new and larger home (including a planetarium). Currently the cylindrical tanks and terrariums of the Steinhart Aquarium put you face-to-face with bug-eyed moray eels and psychedelic-hued frogs. The Natural History Museum combines temporary exhibits (a recent one was on ants) and interactive programmes. It's very kid-friendly, but adults will also be captivated. **Map p. 8, 2C**

Coit Tower 1 Telegraph Hill Blvd., (415) 362-0808. Open 10 am–5 pm daily. No charge for admission; $3.75 for elevator ride to the top. Eccentric heiress Lillie Hitchcock Coit—remembered for her passionate enthusiasm for the city's volunteer fire brigade—bequeathed a part of her fortune to a project that would beautify the city. The money went to this fluted concrete shaft rising from Telegraph Hill; like most distinctive public building projects, it was reviled at first but went on to inspire a whole series of publicly funded building projects during the Depression. The panorama from the top is stunning, but just as interesting—and more important—are the frescoes at the base. Reflecting progressive politics of the 1930s, the murals depict California society in a manner shaped by a sense of the dignity of labour and a deep suspicion of capitalism. It's a wonder these murals survived: they were highly controversial even before their unveiling. (Additional murals on the second floor can be viewed 11 am on Saturday or by appointment.) The student-built website www.coittower.org has details. Take Bus 39 from Washington Square. **Map p. 39, 3B**

Ferry Building www.ferrybuildingmarketplace.com. For most of its history, San Francisco was inaccessible from the north and east except by ship. Millions poured into the city via the ferry terminal— indeed, for a time it was the country's busiest transport station. The 1898 building reflected its importance in suitably grand terms: its tower was modelled on a Seville cathedral and boasted the largest clock dials in the nation (the clock stopped during the exact moment of the 1906 earthquake). In the 1930s, with the opening of the Golden Gate and Bay bridges, ferry traffic dwindled and the building suffered neglect and a humiliating fate as office space. As a final indignity, it was sundered from its natural integration with Market St. by the double-decker Embarcadero Highway. Only with the demolition of the highway and a 2003 renovation did this structure re-establish its connection with the city—and a reinvention as a foodie gathering ground with stalls of organic produce, boutique olive oil, tea and bakery goods. At the water's edge, ferries still depart for Sausalito, Oakland and other points in the Bay. Take Market St. to the water. **Map p. 8, 4B**

Old Mint 88 Fifth St. (at Fifth and Mission). This building, a picture of classic dignity, is the only West Coast example of Greek Revival architecture. When it opened in 1874, the Old Mint was an outpost of the distant Federal government. It manufactured much of the country's coinage and held about a third of the country's gold. Although the 'Granite Lady' survived 1906's earthquake and fire, it's now closed for seismic retrofitting and is slated to reopen in 2007 as a museum of the City of San Francisco. **Map p. 8, 2C**

Transamerica Pyramid 600 Montgomery St. (at Washington). The city's tallest building anchors the skyline with an unmistakable silhouette. The contours of this 1972 insurance company headquarters are not just futurist whimsy—they also

The Transamerica Pyramid

reduce the building's obstruction of the sun and urban views. The skyscraper is not open to the public. **Map p. 8, 2A**

Union Square San Francisco's main square earned its name during the Civil War, when demonstrators rallied here in support of the Union. The square's focal point is a slender column, the Dewey Monument, commemorating the Battle of Manila Bay in the Spanish-American War. Topping the column is the female figure of Victory, but think of her instead as the patron saint of San Francisco art—the young woman who modeled for the statue married a tycoon in the sugar trade and, with her husband, founded the California Palace of the Legion of Honor (see p. 128). Union Square forms the heart of the city's upscale shopping area (for more about Union Square shopping, see p. 39). Maiden Lane, which leads east from the square, now teems with boutiques. But in the late 19th C this street was a raunchy red-light district (something in which San Franciscans take a curious pride). Buses #2, 3, 4, 30, 38 and 45 run to the square. **Map p. 8, 2B**

Chinatown & North Beach

Chinatown is best known for dim sum parlours and crammed-to-the-rafters shops, out of which Buddha figurines, dried fish and other merchandise, both tacky and exotic, spill onto the sidewalk. But San Francisco's Chinatown is more than a colourful neighbourhood; there has been a Chinese community here since 1848 and the development of Chinatown is intrinsically connected to San Francisco history.

Start your exploration on Grant Ave., walking through the Chinatown Gate (at Bush St.; Map p. 8, 2B). Markets where you can buy live animals for your evening meal dominate Stockton St., particularly on Saturdays. Portsmouth Square, today a meeting point for elderly Chinese, is where the US flag was first hoisted in San Francisco in 1846. Wherever you go in Chinatown, glimpses of Chinese associations and senior centres serve as a reminder of the working-class, mainly elderly community that calls this neighbourhood home.

Bargains in Chinatown

For where to eat in Chinatown, see p. 36. To get to Chinatown from Third St., take bus 15; from Union Square, take the Powell Street cable car northbound.

Just past the northern border of Chinatown is North Beach. Once San Francisco's 'Little Italy', later famous for strip joints, the area retains a certain nostalgia also for its coffee-infused Beatnik days. Now it's a local favourite for a stroll and a pastry. Here you'll find mostly cafés and a few old-style Italian restaurants (heavy on the red sauce). For more on where to eat in North Beach, see p. 37.

Grace Cathedral 1100 California St., (415) 749-6300 or (415) 749-6310, www.gracecathedral.org. America's third-largest Episcopal cathedral recalls the medieval Gothic churches of Europe: the facade pays homage to Notre Dame, and the main doors are replicas of those in Florence's Duomo. But much of the interior subverts tradition. How many other houses of worship contain stained-glass windows of Einstein or a mural honouring the United Nations? The church's AIDS Interfaith Chapel (commemorating the victims of the disease) even features an altarpiece by Grafitti artist Keith Haring. Begun in 1928, Grace Cathedral took 36 years to build. Take the California Street cable car. The Powell-Hyde and Powell-Mason cable car lines and buses #1 and 27 also stop nearby. **Map p. 8, 1A**

Nob Hill Nob Hill was the address for the city's rich and powerful. San Francisco's 'Big Four' were Leland Stanford, founder of Stanford University, Collis P. Huntington, Charles Crocker and Mark Hopkins, all tycoons who made their fortunes supplying miners in the 1849 Gold Rush. The Four kept mansions here, although most were destroyed in the fire that followed the 1906 earthquake. The sole survivor, the Flood Mansion, is now an exclusive social club. **Map p. 8, 1A**

The Exploratorium 3601 Lyon St. (at the Palace of Fine Arts), (415) 561-0356, www.exploratorium.edu. Open 10 am–5 pm, Tue–Sun. $12/$9.50 /$8. Free on first Wednesday of each month. Turn yourself into a human battery. Set luminescent bacteria aglow. Watch a chicken embryo develop or a snake decompose. This

Brian Goggin *Defenestration* (1997)

hands-on science museum demonstrates the wonders of physics, biology and sensory perceptions. Kids (and any adult with a sense of fun) will be captivated by the interactive exhibits—you could easily spend an entire afternoon inside this aeroplane-hangar-sized space. Take buses #30, 43, 28, or 29. **Off map p. 39**

Palace of Fine Arts Looking like the ruins of an ancient civilization that never was, the colossal Palace of Fine Arts combines Greek and Roman motifs with its own fantastical elements. The domed pavilion, built in 1915, sits beside a pond complete with swans. For all its pomp, it has a melancholy air, reflected in the sculpted nymphs turning their backs. **Off map p. 39**

Fisherman's Wharf www.fishermans wharf.org. From the Wharf's early days, its fishing boats have brought back the day's catch and served it right on the street. Today steaming cauldrons full of crab still boil along the sidewalks, while behind them stand the area's seafood restaurants, where Italian-style dishes reflect the early fishermen's heritage. Tacky souvenir shops, a wax museum and other shameless tourist-pleasers have since descended on the area, but it's still worth a visit. **Off map**

San Francisco Maritime National Historical Park www.nps.gov/safr The area's seafaring past is also remembered at the free Maritime

Museum on Beach Street (at Polk; off map); the USS Pampanito, a World War II submarine, at Pier 45 (Map p. 39, 1A); and the Hyde Street Pier (at Jefferson; Map p. 39, 1A), with its mini-flotilla of historic ships.

Pier 39 This fanciful two-level shopping attraction packs in the crowds. Musicians and magicians enliven the public spaces, but the biggest attention-grabbers are the sea lions. They turned up on the docks in 1989 and have stayed ever since, barking and throwing around their considerable weight while tourists 'ooh' and 'aah'. Take the Powell-Mason cable car or take bus #15 or 30 from the corner of Kearny and Market. **Map p. 39, 2A**

Defenestration 214 6th St. In 1997, artist Brian Goggin received a grant to throw furniture out the window. Well, not exactly. Defenestration is a site-specific work of wonder and whimsy, transforming a derelict building into art. Chairs clamber out of the windows, pianos hang on by a leg and sofas are definitely on their way somewhere (see picture on previous page). **Map p. 8, 2C**

commercial galleries

Downtown and the Union Square area hold the greatest concentration of galleries in the city, with twenty-two galleries alone on a one-block stretch of Geary St. Many downtown galleries participate in the 'First Thursday' programme, with receptions and extended hours the first Thursday of each month. To the south of Market St. and anchored by SFMOMA and Yerba Beuna, the SoMa area continues to grow as a gallery neighbourhood as well.

49 Geary Galleries This building, once a Western Union building, has enough galleries to keep you busy for an afternoon and is a good place to start in your tour of Downtown's art scene. There are four floors of galleries altogether, so plan to take your time. **Map p. 8, 2B ❶**

Ed Ruscha *L.A.S.F.#1* (2003) at Crown Point Press

Gallery Paule Anglim 14 Geary St. (at Kearny), (415) 433-2710, www.gallerypauleanglim.com. Conceptual art, contemporary paintings, sculpture. Recent exhibits include the political imagery of Enrique Chagoya, sculptures of Deborah Butterfield, and sculpture and drawing by William Tucker. Take BART or Muni to Montgomery St. Station. **Map p. 8, 2B** ❷

Crown Point Press 20 Hawthorne St. (at Howard), (415) 974-6273, www.crownpoint.com. Crown Point Press has hosted an illustrious list of artists, such as Richard Diebenkorn, Ed Ruscha (see previous page) and John Cage, in its 42-year history. Recent shows have been by Richard Tuttle, Shahzia Sikander and Laura Owens. **Map p. 8, 3B** ❸

John Pence Gallery 750 Post St. (between Leavenworth and Jones), (415) 441-1138, www.johnpence.com. Specialising in the work of academic realists, the gallery has a strong stable of contemporary painters and represents significant artists from the 19th–20th C. **Map p. 8, 1B** ❹

John Berggruen Gallery 228 Grant Ave. (between Post and Sutter), (415) 781-4629, www.berggruen.com. Paintings, drawings, sculpture and limited edition prints by regional and international artists such as Richard Diebenkorn, Edward Ruscha, Frank Stella, Georgia O'Keeffe and Wayne Thiebaud. The gallery is owned by the son of famous collector Heinz Berggruen. **Map p. 8, 2B** ❺

Dolby Chadwick Gallery 210 Post St., Suite 205, (415) 956-3560, www.dolbychadwickgallery.com. Representing emerging and mid-career Bay Area painters, both figurative and abstract, including Gary Ruddell, Linda Christensen and Fan Yang. **Map p. 8, 2B** ❺

Meyerovich Gallery 251 Post St., Suite 400, (415) 421-7171, www.meyerovich.com. Specialising in modern and contemporary masters: Picasso, Miró, Chagall, Lichtenstein, Matisse and Motherwell, among others. **Map p. 8, 2B** ❺

Modernism Inc. 685 Market St., Suite 290, (415) 541-0461, www.modernisminc.com. Founded in 1979, Modernism Inc. features international avant-garde from the early 20th C, and contemporary representational and non-representational art. Recent exhibitions include Gottfried Helnwein, Naomie Kremer, Charles Arnoldi. **Map p. 8, 2B** ❷

Weinstein Galleries 383 Geary St.; 353 Geary St.; 337 Geary St.; 253 Grant St., (415) 362-8151, www.weinstein.com. With five galleries in the downtown area, Weinstein shows the work of a wide variety of well-known 20th-C artists—Picasso, Miro, Chagal, and Matisse—as well as established contemporary painters and sculptors. **Map p. 8, 1B** ❻

Hackett-Freedman Gallery 250 Sutter St., Suite 400 (between Grant and Kearny), (415) 362-7152, www.realart.com. Showing a mix of established local artists and the work of moderns such as Louise Nevelson, Milton Avery and Frank Lobdell, among others. **Map p. 8, 2B** ❺

Caldwell Snyder Gallery 341 Sutter St. (at Stockton and Grant), (415) 392-2299, www.caldwellsnyder.com. Calwell Snyder (the gallery has another location in New York) specialises in figurative and abstract works by mid-career European and Latin American painters and sculptors such as Sharon Booma, Alejandro Santiago and José Villalobos. **Map p. 8, 2B** ❼

Jenkins Johnson Gallery 464 Sutter St. (between Powell and Stockton), (415) 677-0770, www.jenkinsjohnsongallery.com. Representing contemporary painting and sculpture, both representational and abstract, by mid-career and established American artists. An annual realism invitational is held each summer. **Map p. 8, 2B** ❽

The Simmons Gallery (formerly Eleanor Austerer) 565 Sutter St. (between Powell and Stockton), (415) 986-2244, thesimmonsgallery.com. Featuring modern art, including work by masters such as Alexander Calder, Picasso, Miró and Chagall. Contemporary artists include Roberto Azank, Vladimir Cora and Michael Rios. **Map p. 8, 1B** ❾

HANG 556 Sutter St. (between Powell and Mason), (415) 434-HANG, www.hangart.com. Hang, and the Hang Annex across Sutter St., feature the work of local and emerging artists. With a wide selection, Hang is an excellent option for beginning and experienced collectors. **Map p. 8, 1B** ❾

Varnish Fine Art Gallery 77 Natoma St. (between 1st and 2nd Sts.), (415) 222-6131, www.varnishfineart.com. Run by two artists, Varnish features contemporary painting and sculpture in an environment designed to be enjoyed, not endured (there's a well-stocked wine bar on site). Recent shows include Bella Feldman, Grant Irish, Craig LaRotonda and Kevin Peter. **Map p. 8, 3B** ❿

Hosfelt Gallery 430 Clementina St. (between 5th and 6th), (415) 495-5454, www.hosfeltgallery.com. Showing abstract and figurative work by contemporary painters, photographers and conceptual artists including Byron Kim, Richard Barnes and Greg Rose. **Map p. 8, 2C** ⓫

Braunstein/Quay Gallery 430 Clementina St. (between 5th and 6th), (415) 278-9850, www.bquayartgallery.com. For over 40 years, Braunstein/Quay has been promoting local artists working with media like clay, fibre and glass—in addition to painting and drawing. **Map p. 8, 2C** ⓫

Andrea Schwartz Gallery 525 2nd St. (at Bryant), (415) 495-2090, www.asgallery.com. Representing emerging and established artists, both local and national, working in paint, photography, installation and sculpture. Recent exhibits include John Belingheri, Tracy Krumm and Gugger Petter. **Map p. 8, 4C** ⓬

New Langton Arts & SF Camerawork 1246 Folsom St. (between 8th and 9th), (415) 626-5416, www.newlangtonarts.org. New Langton and Camerawork share the same space, with Camerawork presenting photography by emerging and mid-career artists looking to push boundaries, and New Langton Arts cultivating experimental contemporary art. **Map p. 8, 1D**

Luggage Store Gallery 1007 Market St. (at 6th), (415) 255-5971, www.luggagestoregallery.com. Presenting cutting-edge work by artists from various cultural and economic communities. **Map p. 8, 1C**

eat

AROUND UNION SQUARE

$$ **John's Grill** 63 Ellis St., (415) 986-3274, www.johnsgrill.com. Open 11 am–10 pm, Mon–Sat; from 5 pm, Sun. This is a beloved San Francisco classic, established in 1908. The look is old and comfortable, with lots of wood and brass, and the small, intimate bar and deep, narrow space make for a cosy refuge from the fog and drizzle. The west wall is covered with photos of famous patrons. This is a meat-and-potatoes, seafood-and-pasta sort of restaurant: the most famous meal ever served here was to detective Sam Spade in Raymond Chandler's novel *The Maltese Falcon*. **Map p. 8, 2B**

Ponzu 401 Taylor St., (415) 775-7979. Breakfast: 7 am–10 am, Mon–Fri, and 8 am–11 am, Sat and Sun. Dinner: 5 pm–10 pm, Mon–Thur, until 11 pm on Fri and Sat. Bar: 5 pm–12 am. The room is full of curves and soft velvet-covered seats, with lots of space and plenty of romantic nooks. The kitchen uses traditional Asian techniques with strictly local ingredients. Try the Thai melon salad with lime leaf, or garlic-fried roti bread with mango chutney. Sour orange-curry sea bass with green papaya and crispy shallots is one of the restaurant's famous dishes, as is stir-fried scallops and duck with spicy black bean greens. **Map p. 8, 1B**

$$$ **Asia de Cuba** Clift Hotel, 495 Geary Blvd., (415) 929-2300, www.clifthotel.com. Open 7 am–11.30 pm. This is in-your-face elegance softened by Old West egalitarianism. The restaurant is

richly panelled in redwood and furnished with plush booths surrounding a T-shaped bar. The men come in anything from jacket to tux and the women are dressed to kill. The name, and the cuisine, are based on the Chino-Latino cookery of pre-Castro Havana. Try *tunapica*, a spicy tartare with currants and almonds in a soy-lime vinaigrette; oxtail spring rolls; lobster potstickers; and crab cakes with shitake mushrooms. **Map p. 8, 1B** ❸

Campton Place 340 Stockton St., (415) 955-5555. Open 11.30 am–10 pm; brunch 11 am–2 pm, Sat–Sun. Understated elegance: it's a study in serenity, designed to let the food take centre stage. The tiny but very lovely bar is a good place to start with a Martini or Cosmopolitan. In the dining room you'll find a frothed foie gras served in a martini glass and a justifiably famous cheese board. The sommelier is always on duty and should be relied on. Campton also serves a legendary breakfast. **Map p. 8, 2B** ❹

Farallon 450 Post St., (415) 956-6969), www.farallon restaurant.com. Open 11.30 am–10.30 pm, Mon–Wed; 11.30 am–11 pm, Thur–Sat; 2.30 pm–10 pm, Sun. Glitz and glamour are said to be particularly American; Farallon bears that out. The fantastic seascape decor usually elicits gasps (mostly of admiration). Jellyfish chandeliers float just beneath the ceiling, a kelp forest is lit from within, and the bar stools rest on octopus legs. It's full of bubble and hubbub, with well-dressed people table-hopping. Seafood lovers should come here at least once to try the roasted walleye pike with English pea ravioli and mint pesto, or giant gulf prawns grilled and served with gnocchi, mushrooms and watercress swimming in sorrel sauce. **Map p. 8, 1B** ❺

Fleur de Lys 777 Sutter St., (415) 673-7779, www.fleurdelysf.com. 6 pm–9.30 pm, Mon–Thur; 5.30 pm–10.30 pm, Fri–Sat. French cuisine and dining in pure, delicious fantasy—you can be forgiven if you think you've just walked onto the set for the movie *The Sheik*, starring Rudolph Valentino, or perhaps fallen into Barbara Eden's genie bottle. Start with a silky lobster bisque or sea scallops with melted leeks, or a simple Serrano ham. Then move to roasted duck breast with cardamom or roasted sea bass in a wine glaze. **Map p. 8, 1B** ❻

Grand Café 501 Geary St., (415) 292-0101, www.grandcafe.net. 11.30 am–2.30 pm and 5.30 pm–10 pm; until 11 pm on Fri and Sat. When you're in the mood to dress to the nines, come here, for the Grand Café is aptly named. Massive columns hold up the decorative ceiling of the former hotel ballroom, which is lit by brilliant chandeliers. The changing menu is Mediterranean-inspired Californian, making extensive use of seasonal vegetables, grilled and roasted meats and fresh fish. Past favourites include wild mushroom tart, Liberty Duck with port and brandied cherries, and sautéed skate wing with braised cabbage. The rich, smooth and buttery mashed potatoes deserve special mention. **Map p. 8, 1B** ❼

Le Colonial 20 Cosmo Place (in the alley between Taylor and Jones, Sutter and Post), (415) 931-3600, www.lecolonialsf.com. Open 5.30 pm–10 pm, Sun–Wed; 5.30 pm–11 pm, Thur–Sat. Shades of French Indochine in this French-Vietnamese restaurant with a 1920s theme. Wander among the rattan couches and chairs, wooden shutters, ceiling fans, and palm fronds and be transported to a bygone colonial era. Upstairs at the bar there's live jazz on Fri and Sat. Most dishes are for sharing—try the crispy spring rolls. The mini crab cakes are a variation on a local favourite, served with a chilli-lime sauce. Reservations recommended. **Map p. 8, 1B** ❽

Scala's Bistro 432 Powell St., (415) 395-8555, www.scalas bistro.com. Open 7 am–12 am, Mon–Fri; from 8 am on Sat and Sun. Located in the historic Sir Francis Drake hotel. Atmosphere is created by the murals, rows of soft leather booths and an open kitchen, with rotisserie in view. It's full of warmth and conviviality, and luscious aromas. The menu changes, but always relies on roasted and grilled meats; the double-cut pork chop with artichokes and roasted garlic is a signature dish. **Map p. 8, 1-2B** ❾

FINANCIAL DISTRICT

$$ **B-44** 44 Belden Lane, (415) 986-6287. Lunch: 11.30 am–2.30 pm, Mon–Fri. Dinner: 5.30 pm–12 am, Mon–Sat. Eating here, in this simple, airy space, it's as if you were in Barcelona, the chef's home town. Even the television in the restroom plays videos from Spain. *Arroz negra*, rice flavoured and dyed with squid ink, is a signature dish. There are also great lamb chops in sherry sauce, or, for vegetarians, *escalivada*. **Map p. 8, 2A-B** ❿

Tadich Grill 240 California St., (415) 391-1849. Open 11 am–9 pm, Mon–Fri; from 11.30 am on Sat. True Gold Rush fare in the oldest restaurant in the city; founded in 1849 and still operated by the same family. Curtained booths line the walls for parties of three or more, while the rectangular bar is there for drinking and solitary diners or couples. The kitchen favours plain cooking and no fancy sauces: grilled seafood and meat and potatoes are the basic fare. Try the Hangtown Fry, basically a frittata of oysters and bacon. **Map p. 8, 3A** ⓫

$$$ **Tommy Toy's** 655 Montgomery St., (415) 397-4888, www.tommy toys.com. Lunch: 11.30 am–2.30 pm, Mon–Fri. Dinner: 5.30 pm–9.30 pm daily. The dining room was fashioned after the 19th-C sitting room of the Empress Dowager of China, and is an orchestration of etched glass, carved wooden arch ways, silvered mirrors, silk draperies and ancient Chinese artefacts. By itself it's a feast for the eyes, but owner Tommy Toy contends that French and Chinese are the greatest cuisines of the world, and his restaurant backs it up. A signature dish is minced squab imperial served in lettuce cups. **Map p. 8, 2A** ⓬

EMBARCADERO

$ **Pier 23** Between Green St and Battery St, (415) 362-5125. 11.30 am–2 am, Mon–Sat; 11.30 am–11 pm, Sun. Sit at the beaten copper bar, have a drink and watch the carnival of shipping and sailing on the bay. Pier 23 was originally a dock worker's bar and grill, and still looks it. The menu is largely fish, steaks and pasta, with sandwiches and burgers available for lunch. In the evenings it hosts popular local jazz bands. There's outdoor dining and drinking on the pier. **Map p. 39, 4B** ⓭

Ferry Building Marketplace At the end of Market St., (415) 693-0996. 10 am–6 pm, Mon–Fri; 9 am–6 pm, Sat; 11 am–5 pm, Sun. The newly renovated and historic ferry building (see p. 22) has been turned into one of the great gastronomic destinations of San Francisco. In addition to purveyors of fresh foodstuffs, wines, chocolates, sausages and so on, some very popular restaurants have located here, with more to follow. **The Slanted Door** is an excellent, modern Vietnamese restaurant; **Taylor's Refresher** is one of the best burger joints in California. **Map p. 8, 4A** ⓮

$$ **Fog City Diner** 1300 Battery St., (415) 982-2000, www.fogcity diner.com. Open 8.30 am–11 pm, Mon–Sat; 1.30 am–10 pm, Sun. 'There is nothing so American as the diner', states Fog City's menu. This smallish and always packed diner calls to mind an Art Deco age. In addition to the standard diner fare such as burgers, sandwiches and meatloaf, you can enjoy Dungeness crab *cioppino*

with prawns and local fish, or macaroni and Gouda cheese with Hobb's ham and English peas. For a light meal try the small plates: crab cakes with capers, seared sirloin capriccio with Bay artichokes and truffle aioli, ahi tuna carpaccio with wasabi cream and daikon sprouts. **Map p. 39, 4B** ⓯

$$$ **Teatro Zinzani** Pier 29, Embarcadero, (415) 438-2668. Open 7.30 pm–11 pm. 'Love, Chaos and Dinner!' is the theme at this musical murder mystery dinner theatre in a gorgeous circus tent. And this is no amateur production; the story line and cast change, but cast members have included John Cleese (of Monty Python fame) and singer Joan Baez. It's a feast of laughter that happens to include a very fine dinner. Dress for the occasion. **Map p. 39, 4A** ⓰

CHINATOWN

$ **Sam Woh** 813 Washington St., (415) 982-0596. Open 11 am–3 am, Mon–Sat. The lunch-time crowd jams into this hole-the-wall, rabbit warren of a restaurant, which spreads over three floors. Atmosphere is ignored and the attitude is summed up in the notice on the wall: 'No credit card, no fortune cookie, just damned good food!' That includes all the basics: chow mein, crisp fried noodles, sautéed shellfish, won ton soup, fried rice. **Map p. 8, 1-2A** ⓱

Yuet Lee 1300 Stockton St. (415) 982-6020. Open 11 am–3 am, Weds–Mon. Another restaurant with nondescript décor and food that keeps patrons coming back. It's a noisy place, serving seafood and noodles to people who know seafood and noodles. The fresh seafood tanks allow you to select your meal on a very personal level, and you can watch through the windows into the kitchen as the chefs render your choice into something wonderful. **Map p. 8, 2A** ⓲

Mon Kiang 683 Broadway St., (415) 421-2015. Open 11 am–10 pm daily. In the region around Hong Kong, Hakka cuisine is peasant cookery. It's hearty and delicious, making maximum use of the least expensive ingredients. This plain but welcoming little place specialises in aromatic salt-baked chicken, which is wrapped in rice paper and buried in a mound of spice-flecked sea salt. The result is uncommonly juicy and flavourful. Also look for pork-stuffed tofu steamed or fried, and heaps of greens. **Map p. 8, 2A** ⓳

Far East Café 631 Grant Ave., (415) 982-3245. Open 11.30 am–10 pm daily. Red-curtained booths line one wall, offering a refuge for spies and lovers. A full bar makes this a good place for early cocktails or one last drink after an evening's fun. The food here is good, if not remarkable, but the atmosphere alone is worth a visit. Also, at these prices it's one of the best deals in town. **Map p. 8, 2A** 🔟

NORTH BEACH

$$ **Moose's** 1652 Stockton St., (415) 989-7800. Open 11.30 am –2.30 pm, Thur–Sat; from 10 am on Sun. On the east side of Washington Square, smack in the middle of North Beach, is one of the pillars of night-time San Francisco, a favourite of politicians, movie stars and everyday folk alike. The menu is Mediterranean-style Californian. The grass-fed beef steaks are excellent, as are the pasta dishes. But the signature dish is California *cioppino*, a rich, tomato-based seafood stew using the local crab and rockfish. Jazz trios play nightly. **Map p. 39, 3B** 🔟

Fior d'Italia 601 Union St., (415) 986-1886, www.fior.com. Open 11.30 am–10.30 pm daily. With a claim to being the oldest Italian restaurant in the nation (established 1886), Fior has a reputation. The small, brightly lit bar opens through storefront windows to Washington Square. In the large and luxurious dining room, leather booths line the walls and circular tables set with heavy cutlery occupy the middle. The menu is old-fashioned 'Italian restaurant' standards. **Map p. 39, 3B** 🔟

SOMA

$ **Yank Sing** 101 Spear St. (One Rincon Center); (415) 957-9300, www.yanksing.com. A cosy space off a side street, all white linens and fine service—not your traditional dim sum. But this is San Francisco; all is well and all is delicious. Choose barbecued pork buns, shrimp moons, silver-wrapped chicken, bits of Peking duck, even a wide variety of vegetarian dim sum, including pea leaves; sautéed eggplant and mustard greens. For a more traditional dim sum experience, try Clement St. (see p. 144). **Map p. 8, 4A** 🔟

$$ **Fringale** 570 4th St., (415) 543-0573. Lunch: 11.30 am– 2.30 pm, Mon–Fri. Dinner: 5:30 pm–10 pm, Mon–Sat. Like stepping into a friend's home in the south of France. The warm and convivial atmosphere is made even more so when the chef stops to share a glass of wine with you. While the menu changes seasonally, you might see pork tenderloin confit with cabbage, onion, and apple marmalade; sautéed prosciutto and sheep's milk cheese terrine; steamed mussels with marinated chopped tomatoes and coriander; bittersweet chocolate truffles. **Map p. 8, 3C** 🔟

Thirsty Bear 661 Howard St., (415) 974-0905, www.thirstybear.com. Lunch: 11.30 am–2.30 pm, Mon–Fri; 12 pm–3 pm, Sat. Dinner: 5.30 pm–10.30 pm, Mon–Thur; 5.30 pm–12 am, Sat; 5 pm–10 pm, Sun. Set in a large, handsome brick building, this festive brewery-cum-Spanish-restaurant takes advantage of its own architecture, with a row of gleaming brewing tanks behind the long bar. There are about a dozen house brews on tap and an excellent wine list. The kitchen turns out various brochettas, shrimp in lemon marinade with artichokes, and *patatas bravas* (fried potatoes made high art). **Map p. 8, 3B** ㉕

Buzz 9 139 8th St, (415) 255-8783. Open 7 am–10 pm, Mon–Wed; 7 am–12 am, Thur and Fri; 9 am–12 am, Sat; 9 am–3 pm, Sun. The hardwood floors show age, the art on the walls shows status as a favourite haunt of local artists and writers (successful ones, that is) and its comfortable banquettes and magazine rack proclaim it as a place where regulars just like to spend time. Serving California cuisine, such as lime and cumin chicken skewers, pan-roasted chicken with a crispy polenta cake, and grilled salmon with a mustard and caper sauce. **Map p. 8, 1D** ㉖

$$$ **Shanghai 1930** 133 Steuart St., (415) 896-5600, www.shanghai1930.com. Lunch: 11.30 am–2.30 pm, Mon–Fri. Dinner: 5.30 pm–10 pm, Mon–Thur; until 11 pm on Fri and Sat. The name says it all. It's designed to look and feel like a subterranean supper club in Shanghai between the wars, and from the gorgeous blue bar to the intimate booths it exudes a slightly sinister elegance. The kitchen turns out dishes like 'ants climbing a tree' (a puffed rice noodle tree with chilli sauce) and the slow-cooked Beggar's Chicken. **Map p. 8, 4A** ㉗

Restaurant LuLu 816 Folsom St., (415) 495-5775. Open 11.30 am–10.30 pm, Sun–Thurs; 11.30 am–11.30 pm, Fri–Sat. A big, stylish place with an open rotisserie kitchen. The centre of the plush dining room is sunken in a conversation pit sort of manner, with a long bar on one side and cocktail tables on another. The 'Cal Mediterranean' menu changes, but rotisserie meats are a constant, as are thin crust pizzas and olive oil mashed potatoes. Roasted mussels are served in a hot iron skillet. **Map p. 8, 3C** ㉘

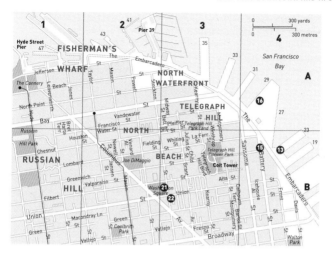

shop

CLOTHES

Anne Fontaine 118 Grant Ave., (415) 677-0911, www.annefontaine.com.
Anne Fontaine may not be a household name in America, but the designer's
white blouses have boosted her to fame in many parts of Europe. These
aren't just white button-downs: some are 17th-C inspired, some have extra-
large, three-tiered collars, and each are tailored to be unique and sexy.
White is a colour of good luck in Fontaine's home country of Brazil. The
boutique also sells soaps, candles, and accessories such as ties, cufflinks,
and even separate sleeves with matching vests. **Map p. 8, 2B** ❶

Anthropologie 880 Market St., (415) 434-2210, www.anthropologie.com.
Founded in 1992, this clothing and housewares chain carries chic labels
like Nanette Lepore as well as one-of-a-kind items such as hand-
beaded cashmeres and hand-built sandals. It's well-stocked for the

home, with everything from couches to candlesticks and plate holders. The store carries some antiques, as well. Design is cheerful and creative; prices are mid-range. **Map p. 8, 2-3B** ❷

Babette 361 Sutter St., (415) 837-1442, www.babettesf.com. Babette has become world-renowned for her pleated raincoats and other pleated clothing. The allure of Babette's women's wear is its portability. The clothing, designed using microfibres, never creases, and can be rolled up for travel and unrolled without looking the worse for wear. The colourful basics can be worn for casual get-togethers or a night at the opera. Durability is an added attraction. **Map p. 8, 2B** ❸

Barcelino Women's at 476 Post St., (415) 912-5700; Men's at 498 Post St., (415) 781-5777. Though Barcelino is based in San Francisco, up to 70% of Barcelino's exclusive designs are manufactured in Europe. The clothing, which is of the highest quality and styled to match, is exclusively sold at Barcelino outlets. In Union Square, the separate men's and women's stores both cater to the business professional, the men's store spotlighting European designers such as Marco Azzali and Belvest, while the women's store, Barcelino Per Donna, taking pride in its formal wear. **Map p. 8, 1B** ❹

bebe 21 Grant Ave., (415) 781-2323; 865 Market St., (415) 543-2323, www.bebe.com. Starting as a San Francisco boutique in 1976, bebe hit big over a decade later with a private collection featuring two originally designed suits. Since then bebe has taken off with hundreds of stores and the full gamut of edgy casual and evening wear. Targeting 18–35-year-olds, the trendy outlet features seductive camisoles and belted tweed trousers. The store also carries its own line of logo-emblazoned casuals as well as accessories. Market St. shop: **Map p. 8, 2B** ❷

BCBG Max Azria 331 Powell St., (415) 362-7360; 865 Market St., (415) 284-9373, www.bcbg.com. BCBG stands for 'bon chic, bon genre', Parisian slang that sums up the philosophy of owner and founder Max Azria. He designs most of the women's clothes for BCBG himself, including the eveningwear and the store's unique, professional suits. His daughter designs the lingerie and swimwear, while his wife also does some designs. Azria continually expands, and has recently taken his BCBGirls fragrance and accessories and turned it into a full sportswear line. He also introduced a line of couture gowns under the name Max Azria Atelier. **Map p. 8, 2B** ❺

Betsey Johnson 160 Geary St., (415) 398-2516, www.betseyjohnson.com. New York designer Betsey Johnson has been fashioning eccentric, youthful clothes since the 1960s. She has since become known for her sexy silhouettes, flowing fabrics, and emphasis on details. This shop shows off her creative flare, with ostrich feather rimmed tops, chiffon dresses, and cashmere cardigans. The prices are not cheap, but the staff is helpful in getting the right style and fit for each customer. **Map p. 8, 2B** ❶

Burberry's Limited 225 Post St., (415) 392-2200, www.burberry.com. Burberry's name will always be associated with its line of trench coats, but the UK-based company, founded in 1856, has expanded its market to emblazon plaid on hats, bathing suits and umbrellas. Founder Thomas Burberry is also credited with inventing the breathable fabric gabardine, but Burberry also produces capes and stoles, children's clothes, men's cashmere sweaters, a line of women's apparel and outerwear, as well as special edition fragrances. Burberry's San Francisco location was recently refurbished, and now covers five floors. **Map p. 8, 2B** ❻

Cicada 547 Sutter St., (415) 398-4000. Cicada takes clothing to the level of art. There are no cookie-cutter designs in this boutique; instead each piece is handmade and unique. Cicada has also gained recognition as a bridal boutique, focusing on artful styles not found in your average bridal magazine. Like a true art space, Cicada changes its fashion displays, often working with local galleries, museums and artists to show works that compliment the clothes. **Map p. 8, 1B** ❼

Couture 395 Sutter St., (415) 781-6915. Couture caters to the business professional with its line of sleek Italian-made clothing. The men's boutique focuses on upscale suits in basic yet stylish cuts, using fine Italian fabrics. The second floor of Couture carries discount prices and overstock. The shop is also an outlet for more casual jackets and sweaters as well as tuxedos. **Map p. 8, 2B** ❽

David Stephen 50 Maiden Lane, (415) 982-1611. David Stephen appeals to the fashion-conscious businessman. Known as the oldest independently owned clothing store in San Francisco, David Stephen debuted in 1969. All the clothes in this men's boutique are made in Italy, mostly by designers like Lorenzini, Canali and Zegna, among others. Look for refined merino wool suits, suede bomber jackets, triple cotton khakis, cashmere and silk polos, and silk ties. **Map p. 8, 2B** ❶

Diana Slavin 3 Claude Lane, (415) 677-9939, www.dianaslavin.com. Slavin's own high-fashion collection runs to muted colours and classic designs like collared, button-down blouses. The store's interior, designed by Diana's husband, architect Robert Baum, provides a retail space and design studio under one roof. Clothes are made on the premises. Closed Sunday and Monday. **Map p. 8, 2B** ❸

Fossil 55 Stockton St., (415) 296-8630, www.fossil.com. Fossil emerged in the 1980s as a watchmaker known for colourful, innovative designs. Since then, Fossil has ventured into other areas, including handbags, belts, backpacks, and even clothes. This shop features a wide array of dress and casual watches in front. It also carries handbags galore, in leather, suede, and other fabrics. Fossil's apparel features mainly denim, faux-vintage T-shirts and other informal attire. **Map p. 8, 2B** 🟡

Georgiou 152 Geary St., (415) 989-8614, www.georgioustudio.com. George Georgiou, who was born in Cyprus, opened his first retail shop in 1974 in Union Square. Georgiou's passion is for elegant, form-fitting pieces, using contemporary colours to accent each creation. While the designs come from San Francisco, the clothes are mostly manufactured in Cyprus. The line ranges from sophisticated suiting and elegant cocktail dress to chic casuals. Prices are actually more reasonable than would be expected of a Union Square boutique. **Map p. 8, 2B** ①

Guess? 90 Grant Ave., (415) 781-1589, www.guess.com. After launching its signature denim wear in the 1970s, Guess? has since branched far and wide from its roots to include women's and men's casual wear as well as a line of kids clothes. Union Square's Guess? shop spans three floors. For the most part, the Guess? styles appeal to teens and twenty-somethings, with prices geared toward that age group. **Map p. 8, 2B** ①

Henry Cotton's 105 Grant Ave., (415) 391-5557, www.henry cottonssf.com. This brand was founded in the 1970s by English golf pro Henry Cotton to outfit European royalty with travel and leisure apparel. Henry Cotton's opened its San Francisco store in 2000. Men's and women's clothes fitting a 'modern country' atmosphere span the store's top two floors. The bottom floor is devoted to outerwear by the French-based Moncler. **Map p. 8, 2B** ①

Jasmin on Maiden Lane 179 Maiden Lane, (415) 393-4589. The atmosphere at this small boutique is casual and inviting, with soft jazz music and comfortable chairs you can sink into to rest your tired-of-shopping feet. Jasmin on Maiden Lane features Italian designer Krizia's urban chic apparel, including cashmere sweaters, hand-embroidered sequin shirts and well-tailored blouses. **Map p. 8, 2B** ⑩

Jin Wang 111 Maiden Lane, #300, (415) 397-9111. Brides-to-be in search of that unique, custom-made gown can empty their pockets at Jin Wang. Wang is renowned for a strong creative flair with wedding dresses as well as devoted personal attention. Aside from the bridal gowns, Jin Wang also makes custom dresses for bridesmaids and the bride's mother, with, of course, accessories to match. **Map p. 8, 2B** ①

Joanie Char 527 Sutter St., (415) 399-9867. Joanie Char's designs gained popularity beginning in the late 1970s, when she opened a wholesale business in San Francisco. Her women's boutique features mostly natural materials, with all items made on the premises. Joanie Char does custom fittings, and patrons can even bring in their own materials. Turnaround time is about a week. The boutique also carries jewellery made by local artists. **Map p. 8, 1B** 7

Japanese Weekend 500 Sutter St., (415) 989-6667. Expectant mothers don't need to sacrifice fashion sense for a full nine months. Japanese Weekend caters to their needs with style and class, offering top-quality designs, whether it's a pair of jeans or a formal dress. The maternity clothes are designed to fit from the early months of pregnancy all the way to a mother's nursing days. Prices here are reasonable. **Map p. 8, 1B** 7

Louis Vuitton 233 Geary St., (415) 391-6200, www.vuitton.com. Louis Vuitton began in the mid-1800s as a luggage designer and later moved onto handbags. After years of expansion, the Paris-based company has moved into apparel, with fashions designed by Marc Jacobs. The prices here rank in the higher ranges, with T-shirts costing over $100 and leather coats over $5,000. **Map p. 8, 2B** 10

North Beach Leather 224 Grant Ave., (415) 362-8300, www.northbeach leather.com. Leather designer Michael Hoban has been garnering attention since the late 1960s for his colourful designs. Whether it's a violet leather skirt, beige leather blazer or red leather pants, Hoban offers much more than the basic black jacket. He's made custom pieces for the Who, Led Zeppelin, Bob Seger, John Lennon and Elvis Presley. Elton John's rainbow fringe jacket and Sammy Davis Jr.'s red, white and blue Captain America outfit are North Beach pieces. **Map p. 8, 2B** 6

Paul Frank 262 Sutter St., (415) 374-2758, www.paulfrank.com. If the name Paul Frank doesn't ring a bell, perhaps the face of Julius the monkey will stir recognition. Julius is the most famous of Paul Frank's many quirky cartoon characters, which appear on everything from T-shirts to visors. Men's and women's clothing are equally bold and fun, using bright colours. For the young in spirit. **Map p. 8, 2B** 3

Prada 140 Geary St., (415) 391-8844, www.prada.com. Prada started as a luggage store, established in Milan in 1913. Now, with her distinctive 1990s style, Miuccia Prada has gained a reputation for quality and design. Shoes are the focus at this upscale boutique. **Map p. 8, 2B** 1

Rolo SoMa 1235 Howard St., (415) 861-4862, www.rolo.com. Think of a hip, trendy designer, and this store will almost surely carry it. Names include Ben Sherman, Cloak, Habitual, Ted Baker and Splendid. This superstore also features men's and women's apparel, skincare items, and assorted accessories. **Map p. 8, 1D** ⓫

St. Croix 651 Market St., (415) 538-8700. Known for its knitwear and sophisticated sportswear, this men's store is a mainstay for Bay Area professionals. The fabrics are wearable and durable, featuring microfibres with a feel that disguises itself as cashmere. Each of the line's famous sweaters is hand-cut, and all are made in limited quantities. **Map p. 8, 2-3B** ❷

St. John Boutique 767A Market St., (415) 856-0420, www.stjohnknits.com. For more than 40 years, the name St. John has been associated with premier-quality knitwear. This store location is expansive, to say the leas: 10,000 square feet. Inside, St. John features sportswear, an elegant eveningwear collection, stylish tailored suits and separates. Using different blends of wool from Australia, St. John appeals to a conservative crowd, though it doesn't shy away from colour. **Map p. 8, 2B** ❾

Ted Baker 80 Grant Ave., (415) 391-1256, www.tedbaker.co.uk. With this store, just opened in 2004, Ted Baker brings his hip, funky line of clothes to the Bay Area. The store has a deer's head on the wall and reading lamps spread about, giving it a sort of manor library atmosphere. There are two limited edition lines in the men's section: the dark and mysterious Phantom line features dinner jackets and dress shirts inspired by the character Dorian Gray. Global is brighter, with splashy coloured jackets and silk print shirts. Ted Baker also offers cufflinks and watches. **Map p. 8, 2B** ❶

The Rafael's 285 Geary St., (415) 956-3489; 643 Market St., (415) 974-6772. The Rafael's describes its selection of clothing as wearable art; more than 40 artists, most hailing from the US, design clothes for the company's two boutiques. Some of the pieces are almost gallery fodder. As for the pricing, think fine art. Geary St. shop: **Map p. 8, 2B** ❺

Thomas Pink 255 Post St., (415) 421-2022, www.thomaspink.co.uk. Designer Thomas Pink built a name for his Jermyn Street shirts and these luxury shirts are a Pink staple. Despite the store's name, there is a kaleidoscope of colours available for Pink's silk ties, as well as its men's and women's shirts. **Map p. 8, 2B** ❻

Three Bags Full 500 Sutter St., (415) 398-SWTR, www.threebagsfull.com. Baa, baa. The shelves in this crammed boutique spill with hand-knit sweaters, mostly from the UK, and funkier designs from Japan. Prices are reasonable, even for the cashmeres: an intricate handmade jacket from Japan can cost $695, while a simple cashmere pullover runs about $130. Bernard and Linda Faber first opened shop in 1979 and now have four locations, three in San Francisco and one in LA. **Map p. 8, 1B** ❼

Wolford Boutique 115 Maiden Lane, (415) 391-6727. Setting the trend in legs, Wolford Boutique offers classic as well as novelty hosiery. Whether it's delicate flowers or bold patterns, the designs are chic and sexy. There are also basics and knit tops. Prices, even for the hosiery, can run high. **Map p. 8, 2B** ❶

SHOES

Allen-Edmonds 171 Post St., (415) 391-4545, www.allenedmonds.com. One of the most unusual aspects of this men's shoe outlet is that the shoes are American-made, rather than hailing from Europe. Anything from loafers to wingtip shoes are available, all in conservative styles and colours. The store carries unusual sizes, too, and any width. Also carries its own Allen-Edmonds cologne and shoe care kits. **Map p. 8, 2B** ⓬

Arthur Beren 222 Stockton St., (415) 397-8900, www.berenshoes.com. This family-run shoe store sells top-of-the-line Italian-made shoes from various designers, such as Antonio Bossi, Salvatore Ferragamo and Bruno Magli. Though shoes are the focus, Arthur Beren also sells watches, bucket hats and stylish handbags. **Map p. 8, 2B** ⓾

Birkenstock 42 Stockton St., (415) 989-2475, www.birkenstock.com. Birkenstock may be associated with its famed foot-hugging, hippie sandals, but the company actually has more than 400 styles and colours of comfort shoes. In addition to the 'Arizona', the sandal that has given Birkenstock its fame, the company offers an array of sandals and clogs with a more stylish, urban look. **Map p. 8, 2B** ❾

Nine West 250 Stockton St., (415) 772-1924, www.ninewest.com. Though the shoes here may not represent the most fashion-forward trends, Nine West offers an array of footwear at bargain prices, and whether it's a formal sandal or casual sneaker, the styles are always up-to-date. **Map p. 8, 2B** ⓾

Ria's Shoes 301 Grant Ave., (415) 834-1420. Foot comfort takes precedence over fashion at Ria's. There is a long list of well-known manufacturers represented, including Timberland, Mephisto, Dr. Martens, Sperry, Birkenstock, Rockport, Clarks of England and Ecco, making Ria's a prime spot for finding a sturdy set of hiking boots or runners. Bargains can be found on the second floor. **Map p. 8, 2B** ⓭

ACCESSORIES

Bottega Veneta 108 Geary St., (415) 981-1700, www.bottega veneta.com. Bottega Veneta's reputation revolves around its artistry with leather, although they sometimes veer into more audacious materials like crocodile or ostrich skin. The line includes sophisticated heels, luggage and bags, wallets, sunglasses. All items are made in Italy, and if there's a weak dollar, it's reflected in the price. **Map p. 8, 2B** ❶

Boucheron 230 Post St., (415) 362-6020, www.boucheron.com. Founded in 1858 by the Boucheron family, the company is credited as the first makers of the wristwatch, the first jewellers to engrave diamonds and combine gold and steel. Today, all Boucheron jewellery is made at the Paris factory. Many celebrities and royalty have worn Boucheron pieces with signature precious metals and stones. **Map p. 8, 2B** ❻

Cecile & Jeanne 255 Grant Ave., (415) 677-0904. Cecile & Jeanne caters to a discriminating clientele with its handmade French jewellery. Hillary Clinton has been photographed wearing one of the shop's brooches, and Carrie from *Sex & the City* wore a piece on the show's final episode. Many pieces are 24-karat gold-plated, with prices ranging from mid-level to 'think before you buy' expensive. **Map p. 8, 2B** ❸

Judith Ripka 110 Geary St., (415) 399-1995. This store serves as an intimate showcase for this New-York-based jewellery artist known for her 18-karat white and yellow gold designs. Ripka, who has been designing since 1969, adds colour to her fine jewellery with semi-precious stones. Items include black onyx earrings featuring 18-karat gold and diamonds and an 18-karat gold chain link ring with a blue quartz cabochon centrepiece trimmed with diamonds. **Map p. 8, 2B** ❶

Kate Spade New York 227 Grant Ave., (415) 216-0880, www.kate spade.com. Kate Spade offers one-stop shopping for matching accessories, whether it be shoes and handbags, knit scarves and hats, or jewellery. Options for bags run the gamut from a pink satin mini-purse with crystal to a chartreuse mid-size suede bag. For men, the Jack Spade line features briefcases, wallets and shoes. Smaller items, including cosmetic cases and body oils, are also sold. **Map p. 8, 2B** ❻

Kati Koos/Smile Gallery 500 Sutter St., Kati Koos (415) 362-3437; Smile Gallery (415) 362-3436, www.katikoos.com. Smile Gallery and Kati Koos share this space as well as sharing a quirky take on life. Kati Koos, which some have labeled 'kooky chic', focuses on bold, colourful clothes and accessories, while Smile plays to the young at heart with its peculiar toys. Kati Koos offers artful items such as lace cardigans and handmade slippers. More funky decorative works include plush velvet cats, paper purses and shoes, and canisters in the shape of chickens. **Map p. 8, 1B** ❼

Metier 355 Sutter St., (415) 986-7603, www.metiersf.com. Metier's claim to fame is its selection of high-end jewellery designed by local artists as well as top names. Cathy Waterman rings and necklaces incorporate 22-karat gold, platinum, diamonds and other precious stones in elegant designs. Metier carries other lines of exquisite jewellery, as well as a clothing section catering to conservative tastes. The designs and labels, such as Development, Rebecca Taylor, and Citizens of Humanity, are not as exclusive as the jewellery. **Map p. 8, 2B** ⓼

Shapur Mozaffarian 335 Powell St., (415) 433-4333. One of San Francisco's finest jewellery shops, Shapur has been in business more than 25 years. Its vast selection includes Chopard diamonds and Hermes and Brequet watches. **Map p. 8, 2B** ⓹

Shreve & Co. Post St. & Grant Ave., (415) 421-2600, www.shreve.com. Shreve first opened its doors in 1852. Though the bright, sprawling interior is less than intimate, the glass cases glitter and sparkle with elegant temptations, including bracelets by Chimento, Cartier watches, diamond band rings by Hidalgo and Shreve-crafted diamond earrings. Other designer lines include watches from Jaeger-LeCoultre and Officine Panerai, pearls by Mikimoto and jewellery by Charles Krypell. **Map p. 8, 2B** ⓺

Tiffany & Co. 350 Post St., (415) 781-7000, www.tiffany.com. First established in 1837 as Tiffany & Young, the name Tiffany has become associated with the finest in diamonds and pearls. Tiffany also garners worldwide recognition for its high-quality engagement and wedding rings, especially its solitaires. **Map p. 8, 2B** ⓾

HOME

Alessi 424 Sutter St., (415) 434-0403, www.alessi.com. Alessi adds a light-hearted touch to any home décor. The Italian-based company creates quirky home items and accessories, such as the Mr. Cold liquid soap dispenser, Dr. Kiss toothbrush, and Origami-style travel bowl for pets by Naoko Shintani. There are also classic designs for practical items, such as the 'Big Shoom' bowl by British architect Nigel Coates and Stefano Giovannoni's hand-held vacuum cleaner. Many items have earned display time in design museums. **Map p. 8, 2B** ⓼

Big Pagoda Company 310 Sutter St., (415) 296-8881. Whether it's a lacquer cabinet from China's Shanxi Province, c. 1950, or a whimsical pig pillow filled with jasmine tea, Big Pagoda caters to eclectic tastes. The store showcases modern, solid-wood furnishings as well as Asian antiques and art. In addition, Big Pagoda carries Japanese stoneware, and glassware and assorted oddities like Kenyan hand-knitted lions made from homespun wool. **Map p. 8, 2B** ⓭

Candelier 33 Maiden Lane, (415) 989-8600. The enticing fragrance that emanates from Candelier is enough to draw in passers-by. Candles are the specialty, in a host of decorative designs. Candelier also carries a large selection of aromatherapy candles. Aside from all the wax, Candelier carries candlesticks and candelabras, as well as a few gift items. **Map p. 8, 2B** 1

Ghurka 170 Post St., (415) 392-7267, www.ghurka.com. Since its inception in 1975, Ghurka has become known as a premiere source for fine leather goods and accessories for travel. The company produces handcrafted alligator handbags, vintage leather wallets, and luggage. Other items include leather glasses cases, manicure sets, hip flasks, and PDA cases. **Map p. 8, 2B** 12

Gump's 135 Post St., (415) 982-1616, www.gumps.com. Many of the items in Gump's hail from the Pacific Rim, including the large Buddha that sits in the middle of this legendary San Francisco store. Founded in 1861 by Solomon Gump as a mirror and frame shop, Gump's specialities still include Jade, Baccarat, Steuben crystal and antiques; you'll also find contemporary crafts, bedding and towels, and garden ornaments and accessories. Another big draw is artistic glass from Italian-born Lino Tagliapietra. There are also basic home, furniture and bath items, as well as unusual decorative art, like statues of Qing Dynasty emperors and brass bulldog doorstops. **Map p. 8, 2B** 12

Sanrio Superstore 865 Market St., in the basement of the San Francisco Centre, (415) 495-3056, www.sanrio.com. Sanrio takes Japanese whimsy to the max, with crazily coloured toys and items of dubious practical use. The furniture, bags, watches, notebooks and other items all feature characters such as Hello Kitty and Chi Chi Monchan. The slightly more functional items include Hello Kitty wallets and key rings, Cinnamoroll drinking glasses, plush toys, Hello Kitty milkshake makers and Hello Kitty portable TVs. **Map p. 8, 2B** 15

Sur La Table 77 Maiden Lane, (415) 732-7900, www.surlatable.com. If there is anything missing from your kitchen, Sur La Table is sure to have it. The vast selection includes tortilla warmers, bake ware, kitchen furnishings and cookbooks. Seattle-based Sur La Table also specialises in speciality foods such as cocktail elixirs, chocolate fondue sauce and champagne vinegar. **Map p. 8, 2B** 1

GIFTS AND MISCELLANEOUS

Adolph Gasser 181 2nd St., (415) 495-3852, www.gassers.com. Since 1950, Adolph Gasser's store has been a lifeline for photographers in the

Bay Area ever since. The store sells a wide array of new and used equipment in all formats, as well as books on photography, tripods, camera backpacks, and other photography accessories. Prices here can be a bit higher than in other San Francisco camera shops, but the service is excellent. **Map p. 8, 3B** 16

Caswell-Massey 372 Sutter St., (415) 296-1054, www.caswell massey.com. Believed to be the fourth-oldest company in America, Caswell-Massey began as an apothecary shop selling medical supplies. Caswell-Massey's Number Six Cologne was actually a favourite of President George Washington. This old-world apothecary brims with traditional aromatic fragrances, grooming products, soaps and body essentials. Caswell-Massey carries its own line of bath products, fragrances, bath gels, lotions and gift baskets. **Map p. 8, 2B** 9

Diptyque 171 Maiden Lane, (415) 402-0600, www.diptyqueusa.com. Diptyque has been making natural scents for over 45 years, presenting them in a variety of ways—most famously through its candles. Some of the popular fragrances for candles and room sprays include Baies (black currant leaves and Bulgarian roses), tuberose, fig tree, and lavender leaf. Body perfumes such as Oyedo—citrus fruits and thyme—are also popular. Diptyque diversifies with books, jams, jellies and teas, and Eskandar brand bath essences, milks, body washes and soaps. **Map p. 8, 2B** 10

Kar'ikter 418 Sutter St., (415) 434-1120, www.karikter.com. When Kar'ikter debuted in 1995, it was the first store in the US to pay homage to Belgian cartoon character Tintin with books and other paraphernalia. The shop still carries Tintin items, but also goods featuring Le Petit Prince, Asterix, Babar, Wallace & Gromit, the Smurfs and Noddy. Kar'ikter also carries Alessi and odd knick-knacks such as Philippe Starck's gnomes. **Map p. 8, 2B** 8

Lush 240 Powell St., (415) 693-9633. Lush is a state of mind, and at this bath and cosmetics store it's a bodily state as well. The bright and cheerful UK-based company specialises in pleasure focusers such as bath bombs, creamy candy bath melts, hot toddy bubble bars and dream-catcher massage bars. The ingredients include essential oils and other all-natural items, and everything is fresh. **Map p. 8, 2B** 17

The Tumi Store 100 Grant Ave., (415) 402-0820, www.tumi.com. Named after a Peruvian god, Tumi fashions its luggage with both business and leisure travellers in mind. Soft-sided, wheeled carry-on bags and durable overnight bags are excellent, as are the passport holders, small folding travel packs and garment bags. Business travellers can find scratch-resistant leather briefcases, leather cell phone holders and computer bags. The store is known for the superb quality of the materials and its functional, innovative creations. **Map p. 8, 2B** ❶

The Whisky Shop/Hector Russell Scottish Imports 360 Sutter St., (415) 989-1030; (415) 989-5458, www.whiskyshopusa.com; www.hector-russell.com. Whisky aficionados will find a piece of heaven at the Whisky Shop, which boasts more than 400 whiskies. Malt whiskies are the speciality, including 40–50-year-old rare malts that can fetch $2,000. Also residing within the shop is Hector Russell Scottish Imports, featuring a wide selection of kilts, some hand-stitched, as well as Tartan trousers, kilt jackets and mini-kilted skirts for women. All items in the store are imported from Scotland. Kilts can also be rented. **Map p. 8, 2B** ❽

Jeffrey's Toys 685 Market St., (415) 243-TOYS. Not just for kids; even adults will find treasures at Jeffrey's. This independent toy store features toys for small children, stuffed animals, dolls, Homies toys and classic board games. There are also comics, action figures and a full set of Schleich figures, as well as electronic games. **Map p. 8, 2-3B** ❷

BOOKS

Rand McNally Map and Travel Store 595 Market St., (415) 777-3131. This store can be dangerous for anyone with even the slightest travel bug. Shelves are filled with every guidebook imaginable (we recommend art/shop/eat and Blue Guides, of course), as well as travelogues and related titles. It is also stocked with maps, atlases, globes, and travel gear including backpacks, toiletry kits, neck pillows for long flights, money pouches, adapters and travel hair dryers. **Map p. 8, 3B** ❿

Stacey's Bookstore 581 Market St., (415) 421-4687, www.staceys.com. Opened by John W. Stacey in 1923, this bookshop started with just 400 books. Now it's a superstore, one of the largest bookstores in San Francisco. On the three floors are over 150,000 books, including a large selection of professional and technical titles. Stacey's is known for its author events, with both fiction and nonfiction writers holding readings and signings. It's also a good place for autographed stock. **Map p. 8, 3B** ❿

THE MISSION DISTRICT

Precita Eyes Mural Project

OPEN	10 am–5 pm, Mon–Fri; 10 am–4 pm, Sat; 11 am–4 pm, Sun
CHARGES	**One-hour tour** $10 adults, $8 college students, $5 seniors, $2 children (under 18). **Extended tour** $12 adults, $8 college students, $5 seniors, $2 children (under 18)
GUIDED VISITS	On Saturday the one-hour tour meets at Café Venice (3325 24th St., at Mission) at 11 am; on Sunday it meets at Precita Eyes at 11 am. The extended tour meets at Precita Eyes every Saturday and Sunday at 1.30 pm.
TELEPHONE	(415) 285-2287
WEB	www.precitaeyes.org
MAIN ENTRANCE	2981 24th St. (at Harrison)
GETTING THERE	Take BART to 24th St. Station

San Francisco is home to more than 1,000 murals— the Mission District, the traditionally Latino neighbourhood of the city, contains the highest concentration. The murals do more than decorate; they reflect the history, traditions, and life of this part of the city and are an important symbol of cultural pride. Precita Eyes Mural Project, a not-for-profit organisation devoted to promoting, creating, and protecting this outdoor art form, offers guided walking tours of the murals— more than 80 of them in a six-block area. The longer tour includes an introduction to the history of mural-painting and the connection between murals and Mexican culture, starting from the early 1900s and including the great muralists Diego Rivera, David Alfaro Siqueiros, and José Clemente Orozco. The shorter tour is only a walking tour. Bicycle and bus tours can also be arranged.

THE MURALS

For those looking to explore the murals on their own, *Balmy Alley*, which cuts from 24th and 25th Sts., between Harrison and Treat, is a good first stop. This small alley is decorated on both sides with a series of colourful murals—40 in all—painted by different artists. The oldest date back to 1972, and many more were painted in the 1980s; political events of the time in Central America influence the subject matter in many of them. At the far end of the alley a large image of a child's eyes reflects the tiny figure of a soldier and a white dove of peace. A more recent mural by **Joel Bergner**, titled *Un Pasado que qun Vivre*, reflects daily life in El Salvador in vivid reds and yellows, with the memories of violence as constant shadows.

Walking east on 24th St., you will encounter a number of other murals. One particularly noteworthy mural is on the side of St Peter's Church, on the corner of 24th St. and Florida. It was painted by **Isaias Mata**, a professor from San Salvador jailed during the 1980s for activism, and dedicated in appreciation for the help he received from the church during this time. In bright colours and bold design, it depicts five centuries of aggression against the native peoples of Central America, and five hundred years of resistance. On the corner of 24th St. and York is another

mural of monumental proportions and strong political leanings. La Llorona is a Latino legend of the weeping woman, shown here in the centre of the mural. The artist, **Juana Alicia**, has brought a modern twist to an old story and embedded various scenes into the larger design: in the upper left you'll see a bloated man with water spouting out of him. On the soles of his shoes, note the logo for the American company Bechtel, which buys water rights in developing countries. In the lower left is a scene from India, where a proposed dam project has displaced an entire village. Alicia's political themes run throughout this mural done in shades of blues and reds.

in the area

Mission St. This is the main street of the Mission District. If you're not going down south of the border, this is the next best thing, filled with little shops stocking Jarritos guava soda, and vendors that sell mango with chili or tamales from pushcarts. It's a real neighbourhood—not yet spruced up in the city's wave of inexorable gentrification, although it has a distinctly visible boho population—and has an atmosphere all its own. **Map p. 52, 3B to 3-4 C**

Clarion Alley 24th St. is not the only place to find murals in the Mission. Those looking for murals in the northern section of the district should take a walk down Clarion Alley, which cuts from Valencia to Mission Sts., between 17th and 18th. Starting from the early 1990s, a group of residents of the alley decided to begin painting. Now, more than ten years later, Clarion Alley resembles an outdoor museum of street art, and a sunny day may find several muralists hard at work. There is constant turnover and new projects are always developing. The original group of muralists oversees the project, though not all live on the alley now. Aspiring muralists submit their designs to the group, which has the final say on approving new work. The community even holds an annual block party on the alley each autumn as a celebration of art and community. Take the #14 Valencia bus to 17th St. **Map p. 52, 2-3C**

Mission Delores Corner of 16th and Delores, (415) 621-8203. Open 10 am–4 pm, Mon–Sun. Admission $2. It takes all one's imagination to picture Mission Delores as it was two-hundred-odd years ago: a lonely outpost of Spanish Catholicism on the North American frontier. The mission, officially known as San Francisco de Asís, celebrated its first mass on June 29, 1776 (just as colonial settlers on the other side of the continent were preparing to declare independence from Britain). The mission building went up in 1791, which makes it San Francisco's oldest surviving structure. Built from adobe bricks, it survived the 1906 earthquake (the church next door did not—a replacement was built in 1913). The question is posed in the mission's museum today: was Delores a Spanish mission or an Indian town? The adjacent cemetery, a cypress-shaded garden spot, contains the graves of early settlers. From Union Square, take the J streetcar south down Market St. **Map p. 52, 2A-B**

The Castro - Map p. 52, 1A

Today's epicentre of queer power was once a sleepy working-class suburb. In the late 1960s the Castro saw its first significant influx of gay men, who restored the area's then affordable Victorian houses. The population eventually reached critical mass; the rainbow flag flies proudly, and bars that once sheltered an alternative lifestyle now flaunt it.

The Castro Theatre is a neon landmark of the district, just off Market St. (www.thecastrotheatre.com). A 1922 movie palace, built as a gaudy Art Deco vision of Neo-Hispanic splendour, it's still a popular neighbourhood cinema. The theatre programming is a typically San Franciscan mix of art-serious and pop-fun, running childhood favourites, small films from around the world and giants of cinema history.
To get to the Castro, from Market St. take the F or S streetcar southwest to the end of the line.

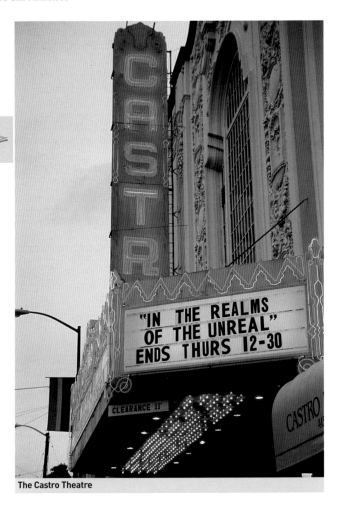

The Castro Theatre

commercial galleries

Mission Cultural Center for Latino Arts 2868 Mission St., (415) 821-1155, www.missionculturalcenter.org. Call for hours and exhibits. Established in 1977 to promote the arts and culture of Chicano, Central and South American and Caribbean peoples, the Mission Cultural Center for Latino Arts offers a series of art exhibits that draws upon and preserves this heritage. Many of their gallery shows are at the Meridian Gallery (545 Sutter St., Suite 20), but the centre also has its own gallery, and mounts an annual Day of the Dead show each November, curated by a local artist. Take BART to 24th Street Station. **Map p. 52, 4C** ❶

Blue Room Gallery 2331 Mission St., (415) 282-8411, www.blueroom gallery.org. The Blue Room Gallery may be the first mainstream gallery located in the heart of the Mission. With two floors of exhibition space, Blue Room features themed exhibits—including an annual Bay Area Furniture Art show each fall—as well as work by artists such as Oscar Camilo De Las Flores, Donald Fortescue and Florian Roeper. The gallery also serves as a performance space. Take bus #14 Mission to 20th St. **Map p. 52, 3B** ❷

SomArts Cultural Center 934 Brannan St., (415) 863-1414, www.somarts.org. The SomArts Cultural Center is a non-profit arts centre that houses a number of organisations, including Artspan, responsible for the annual October series of Open Studios throughout the Bay Area. The gallery space at SomArts features a preview of the event, showing work by different participating artists. Take bus #19 Polk to Brannan St. **Off map**

Intersection for the Arts 446 Valencia St., (415) 626-2787, www.theintersection.org. As San Francisco's oldest alternative art space, Intersection features a gallery of rotating themed exhibitions as well as performance space for a variety of emerging and established artists. Each exhibition is paired with events that further explore the theme and provide for an interactive, interdisciplinary art experience. Take BART to 16th Street Station. **Map p. 52, 3A** ❸

Artist-Xchange 3169 16th St., between Valencia & Guerrero, (415) 864-1490, www.artist-xchange.com. This cheerful gallery features local artists working on a wide variety of fine and functional art, from paintings and photography to blown glass, jewellery, pottery and stationery. Take BART to 16th Street Station. **Map p. 52, 3A** ❹

Encantada Gallery of Fine Art 904 Valencia St. (at 20th), (415) 642-3939. This bright and colourful gallery and shop specialises in the arts and crafts of Mexico. The gallery rotates eight shows a year. Take bus #26 Valencia to 20th St. **Map p. 52, 3B** ❺

Jack Hanley Gallery 395 Valencia St. (at 15th), (415) 522-1623, www.jackhanley.com. The focus is on contemporary art in this small gallery (formerly located in the downtown area). Artists represented include Erwin Wurm, Xylor Jane, Simon Evans and Anne Collier. Take BART to 16th Street Station. **Map p. 52, 3A** ❻

City Art Gallery 828 Valencia St., (415) 970-9900, www.cityartgallery.org. Voted best gallery in an annual newspaper poll three years running, this cooperative gallery features a wide variety of work by local artists. Openings are the first Friday of each month. Take bus #26 Valencia to 19th St. **Map p. 52, 3B** ❼

Galeria de La Raza 2857 24th St. (near Bryant), (415) 826-8009, www.galeriadelaraza.org. A non-profit, interdisciplinary space for art, thought, and activism, the gallery and adjoining Shop 24 focus on promoting public awareness and appreciation of Chicano/Latino art and culture. Offers rotating exhibitions as well as films and spoken word presentations. Take BART to 24th Street Station or bus #14 Mission to 24th St. **Off map**

Creativity Explored 3245 16th St., (415) 863 2108, www.creativity explored.org. Creativity Explored is a non-profit visual arts centre for adults with developmental disabilities. Recent exhibition themes include 'Spirits and Saints', an annual holiday show, and 'Fired and Wired', a show that featured computer graphics and ceramics. Take BART to 16th Street Station. **Map p. 52, 3B** ❽

Southern Exposure Gallery at Project Artaud 401 Alabama St. (at 17th), (415) 863-2141, www.soex.org. Since 1974, Southern Exposure has been committed to new and diverse, risk-driven art. In its 2,400 square feet of exhibition space the gallery has presented solo shows for artists including John Beech, Rene de Guzman, Marisa Hernandez, Melissa Pokorny, Maria Porges and Armando Rascon. Take bus #22 Filmore to Harrison St. **Off map**

The Lab 2948 16th St (between Mission and Capp), (415) 864-8855, www.thelab.org. Founded in 1984 by a group of interdisciplinary artists, the Lab is known for experimental work by emerging artists. There are four to six gallery shows each year. The Lab hosts a popular 'postcard show' each November, featuring reasonably priced, small-format works. Take BART to 16th Street Station. **Map p. 52, 4A** ❾

Crucible Steel at CELLspace 2050 Bryant St., (415) 648-7562, www.cellspace.org. Housed in the non-profit art space Collectively Explorative Learning Labs (CELLspace), Crucible Steel Gallery features emerging local artists and holds a biannual open 'call for art'. It is wise to call ahead and find out what is on at the gallery. Take bus #27 Bryant to 18th St. **Off map**

eat

$ **El Nuevo Fruitlandia** 3077 24th St., (415) 648-2958. Open 11.30 am–3 pm and 5 pm–9pm, Tue–Fri; from 12 pm–10 pm, Sat and Sun. This small, unpretentious Puerto Rican establishment is one of the stars of the Mission district. It's been here for as long as anyone remembers, serving rich, hearty fare at very reasonable prices. Let the very friendly staff serve you such house specialities as roast pork with rice and yucca; any one of a variety of plantains; chicken in green sauce; shredded beef with peppers; Puerto Rican dumplings; or shrimp in garlic sauce. Very popular as a snack or a take-away are *batidos de frutas*, thick fruit shakes. **Map p. 52, 4C**

La Palma Mexica-tessen 2884 24th St., (415) 647-1500. Open 10.30 am–9 pm, Sun–Fri; 11.30 am–9 pm, Sat. Billed as a 'Mexican delicatessen', La Palma is a grocery shop with a take-away counter where you can get superb handmade tamales, as well as other Mexican street food. Mission-style burritos are a meal unto themselves and the tacos make a fine snack. If you're staying with friends or in an apartment where you can cook, this is the place to buy the ingredients for your own in-house fiesta. **Off map**

St Francis Fountain 2801 24th St., (415) 826-4200. Open 11 am–9 pm, Mon–Fri; 11.30 am–8 pm, Sat–Sun. A very traditional old-time soda fountain, with stools at the counter and an old storefront. In operation since 1918, it's a Mission institution. The main attraction here is ice cream and malted milk shakes, the kind enjoyed by earlier generations. For those wanting a proper lunch there are burgers and sandwiches on the menu. You can even order an old-fashioned egg cream soda. **Off map**

Rite Spot Café 2099 Folsom St., (415) 552-6066. Open 7 pm–11 pm, bar open until 2 am. This is a true old neighbourhood joint in the middle of a hip and happening block. Small, dark and intimate, you can almost touch the bar from any table. Come for a simple menu of pasta, steak or meatloaf with mashed potatoes and gravy, washed down with cheap red wine. Live Tin Pan Alley music most nights. **Map p. 52, 4B** ❹

$$ **Luna Park Kitchen and Cocktails** 694 Valencia St., (415) 553-8584, www.lunaparksf.com. Open 11.30 am–10.30, Mon–Thur; until 11.30 pm, Sat; until 10 pm, Sun. The small storefront entrance opens onto an airy room with dark maroon walls, and deep booths under crystal chandeliers. The open kitchen keeps things warm and aromatic. The restaurant specialises in 21st-C comfort food: fried wonton chips, pork cutlet stuffed with mushrooms and Gruyere, brisket. **Map p. 52, 3B** ❺

Ramblas Tapas Bar 557 Valencia St., (415) 565-0207. Open 5 pm–11 pm, Sun–Thur; until 1 am, Fri–Sat. Named after Barcelona's famous street, with heavy wooden chairs and tables for the feel of a Spanish inn. Wide windows in front make for good people watching. Notable on the menu are fat stalks of asparagus marinated and grilled and pork skewers lightly spiced. The only plate that isn't small is *patatas bravas*, chunks of potato deep fried and served with a piquant tomato salsa. **Map p. 52, 3B** ❻

Last Supper Club 1199 Valencia St., (415) 695-1199. Open 5.30 pm–10.30 pm. It's dark, cramped and crowded in here—but that's a good thing! This is one of the happiest and most comfortable places in town. The antipasti plate is a work of art; the chestnut ravioli are creamy; the pork osso buco is fall-apart tender. **Map p. 52, 3C** ❼

Levende Lounge 1710 Mission St., (415) 864-5585, www.levendesf.com. Open 5 pm–11 pm, Tue–Fri; from 6 pm on Sat. Step inside then stop, look and listen. On the opposite wall is the colourful long bar. To your left is the dance floor, surrounded by lounge furniture. Along the walls are the dinner tables, and at the far side the DJ spins on one of the most sophisticated sound systems in town. Check out the cocktail menu before the dinner menu. Then look at the fusion/eclectic fare and try beau soleil oysters or horseradish-yuzu mignonette to start, then *tilapia ceviche* or duck confit tacos. **Map p. 52, 3A** ❽

$$$ **Foreign Cinema** 2534 Mission St., (415) 648-7600. Open 5.30 pm–11 pm, Tue–Sat; cinema and bar stay open until 2 am. In a soaring space with impossibly high ceilings, wooden tables surround a central fireplace and a semi-open kitchen. Outside, on the patio, diners watch a film (foreign, naturally) projected on the wall of the building. The menu changes frequently to match the whim of the chef and what's seasonal best of California's justifiably famous produce. **Map p. 52, 3-4C** ●

shop

THRIFT & VINTAGE

Clothes Contact 473 Valencia St., (415) 621-3212. With the same owner as Mission Thrift (below), Clothes Contact has a similar stock of used jeans, shirts, coats and other basic items. Most of the clothes here are sold by the pound, except for a few higher-priced items, such as the leather jackets. Vintage brocade and velvet are also sold by the pound. There are also cheap wigs behind the counter. **Map p. 52, 3A-B** ●

Community Thrift Store 623 Valencia St., (415) 861-4910. Taking up a large expanse of this Mission District block, the Community Thrift Store stocks anything and everything imaginable. This is the spot for used records, clothes, costumes, furniture, kitchenware, books, toys, home appliances and more. There are damaged goods as well as merchandise in decent condition, but the prices are always right. What differentiates this thrift store from all the rest is its community participation. The goods are all donated by the public, and the proceeds benefit local charities, with donors deciding the charity of their choice from a list of over 200, everything from AIDS organisations to groups assisting battered women. **Map p. 52, 3B** ●

Mission Thrift 2330 Mission St., (415) 821-9560. One of the better used-clothing shops in the Mission, this store is a lively spot where you can sift through racks and racks of clothing. Aside from the usual shirts, skirts, sweaters and jeans, this shop offers a variety of accessories, including tutus and wigs. There is a wall of toys behind the counter. **Map p. 52, 4B** ●

Out of the Closet 2415 Mission St., (415) 550-1599. One of several Out of the Closet thrift stores in San Francisco. This location sells everything from clothing to old stereos, fax machines, sofas, chairs and microwaves. The clothes couldn't be much cheaper, with deals like five pieces for $10. One of the features is this store's wall of used books. Proceeds from purchases directly benefit medical care provided by the AIDS Healthcare Foundation. **Map p. 52, 4B** ④

Retrofit Vintage 910 Valencia St., (415) 550-1530. Retro says it all in this sassy shop. Vintage wear from the 1950s through the 1980s runs the gamut from beaded gowns to basic shirts. One of the store's top sellers is a new T-shirt that can be emblazoned with retro transfers, such as the Atari logo or images from old David Bowie album covers. The store is filled with wigs, hats, shoes, ties, and buttons that say Gucci, Pucci, Dior, Rubik, and other old-school labels. There are occasionally DJs spinning, making shopping all the more fun. **Map p. 52, 3B** ⑤

Something Very Special 2417 Mission St., (415) 821-2321. Most of the clothes at this thrift shop are used but in good condition. Young bargain shoppers and many of the locals flock here for the deals as well as the large selection of colourful costume jewellery in front. **Map p. 52, 4B** ④

Schauplatz 791 Valencia St., (415) 864-5665. Fun, flashy vintage wear has been the speciality at Schauplatz for nearly six years. The bulk of the items are from the 1960s and 1970s, though the stock spans the 20th C. Women's and men's used clothes are elegant to everyday, including suits, blazers, shirts, and skirts. The stock always changes, but it's not uncommon to find treasures such as a 1930s Shanghai silk dress or a 1950s Mexican wool jacket. **Map p. 52, 3B** ⑥

Thrift Town 2101 Mission St., (415) 861-1132, www.thrifttown.com. Thrift Town reigns as the largest of the Mission's thrift stores. The main floor features clothes, children's toys and clothing, shoes and accessories, while the upstairs has furniture and housewares, among other items. The immensity of the store and the slightly chaotic atmosphere may make it a bit off-putting, but the bargain prices mean Thrift Town is well worth the hunt. In addition to the everyday low prices, every Mon night there's a '30% off' sale on clothes. **Map p. 52, 3B** ②

CLOTHES

Dema 1038 Valencia St., (415) 206-0500, www.godemago.com. Casual, hip, and certainly colourful, Dema Grim has been on the cutting edge of the San Francisco retro fashion look since opening her store in 1997.

SHOPPING IN THE MISSION DISTRICT

She sticks to 1960s-inspired simple shapes and forms, but adds an artistic flair with colours and patterns. Some of her designs include a Flower Power straight wool coat and form-fitting vintage-style blouses. The shop also carries accessories, as well as some clothes by other like-minded designers. **Map p. 52, 3C** 7

Foxy Lady Boutique 2644 Mission St., (415) 285-4980, www.foxylady boutique.com. This is the spot for ladies interested in flashing their foxy side. Though women can find formal dresses and basic clothes, this store specialises in sultry lingerie as well as sexy skirts and blouses. There is plenty of mesh, lycra, lace, chiffon and fishnet to choose from, with an emphasis on baby doll sets. Sexy costumes for Halloween or just fun at home. Closed Mondays. **Map p. 52, 4C** 8

Hats 758 Valencia St., (415) 255-2787, www.adshats.com. We're not just talking baseball caps, here; this hat shop carries over 8,000 types, from cashmere rollups to top hats, berets to crocheted caps, fedoras to animal-shaped kids' hats. Fashionable, fun, and funky are the keywords, and even the rain hats are decorative. A variety of designers are represented, but co-owner Elina Davenport, who runs the shop with her brother, makes 30% of the stock under the label Alternative Design Studio. **Map p. 52, 3B** 4

House of Hengst 924 Valencia St., (415) 642-0841. The women's section is all Hengst wear, designed in-house by Susan Hengst, while the men's carries the 'hrm' label, designed in nearby beach town Santa Cruz by Bob Scales. The women's side features a smart line that can be worn for any occasion. The clothes have a bit of wild, such as a gold knit snap-front jacket, a fuchsia wool jacket or pink nylon sleeveless dress. For men, the clothes run from casual to dress, with primary or muted colours and several classic plaids. **Map p. 52, 3B** 5

Laku 1069 Valencia St., (415) 695-1462, www.lakuyaeko.com. Laku (the word means 'happy' or 'comfortable' in Japanese) opened in 1993 as one of the first alternative shops in the Mission. Every item in the store is original and handmade. As a matter of fact, it's common to see designer Yaeko Yamashita working away in back of the shop. Some items include colourful men's, women's, and children's slippers; knit, straw, and French-trim hats; yoga bags; aprons; and other gift items. Fabrics, such as silk, cotton, velvet and brocade, are mostly vintage. **Map p. 52, 3C** 7

Marian's 2040 Mission St., (415) 863-5897. This clothing shop is divided into sections. 'Missy merchandise' is geared toward women ages 30 to 60. The other side houses a basic men's selection with some known labels, including Timberland, Calvin Klein, and Levi's. While the men's clothing runs in regular sizes, the women's focuses on plus sizes, starting from size 10 and up. There are no big designers represented, but the selection is varied and the prices low- to mid-range. **Map p. 52, 3C** 9

Otsu 3253 16th St., (415) 255-7900, www.veganmart.com. Yvonne Chen and Jeremy Crown opened this vegan boutique in 2002. All products are made without animal products. Its small stock of shoes is imported from England and Australia, while the shop also carries non-leather belts, wallets and handbags. Otsu is a Japanese word that translates as 'stylish, chic, quaint, strange, tasty, delicious'. The store also carries hand-knit hats, vegan cookbooks, independent 'zines, CDs recorded by the owner's acquaintances, recycled paper products, handmade gift items and its own limited-edition shirts. **Map p. 52, 2-3B** 10

Siegel's Clothing Superstore 2366 Mission St., (415) 824-7729, www.zootsuitstore.com. A haven for hepcats and swing music fans, this men's clothing store specialises in retro wear, including 1930s and 1940s era zoot suits. Siegel's, which outfits many of the world's swing ensembles, offers off-the-rack suits as well as custom-made outfits. Men can find all the accessories, including silk ties, cufflinks and zoot chains. Other store items include suspenders, jeans, retro KISS shirts, outerwear and construction pants. There is also a tux rental shop in back. **Map p. 52, 4B** 3

Sunhee Moon 3167 16th St., (415) 355-1800, www.sunheemoon.com. Designer Sunhee Moon, who has fashioned clothes for major department stores like Barney's, New York, takes inspiration from the tailored clothes of the 1950s. Her shop carries basics with fun details, such as button-up blouses with unusual buttons. Stretch and comfort are emphasised in the styles and fabrics, such as Pima cotton shirts and wool jerseys. This boutique carries jewellery from local designers as well as stylish handbags and hair clips. **Map p. 52, 3A-B** 11

Weston Wear 584 Valencia St, (415) 621-1480, www.westonwear.com. Weston Wear is an outlet for designer Julie Weston's line of nylon prints. Her women's clothes are renowned for their comfortable stretch, making them ideal for all sizes, even pregnant women. Her sexy, colourful line includes hip-slung skirts, shrug tops and more. The shop offers high-discount sales twice a year. Aside from Weston's own clothes, the store carries jewellery and handbags by various designers. **Map p. 52, 3B** 2

SHOES

Bonita Trading Co. 2512 Mission St., (415) 642-0811. This store is dubbed 'The Family Shoe Store' for good reason: the small space is jammed with an enormous stock of shoes, from basic sneakers to fashionable boots. There is nothing fancy here—most of the shoes are geared toward kids, including girls' dress-up sandals in all styles and colours. **Map p. 52, 4C** 12

Queen's Shoes 2356 Mission St., (415) 285-1855. One of the longest-running shoe stores, around since 1969. The store is not flashy, and could easily be missed, but it does carry many inexpensive name brands of shoes and sneakers. Some of the labels include Dockers, Dickies, Adidas and Skechers. It is very low key, so there is no pressure if you want to try stuff on. Lots of sales. Closed Wednesday. **Map p. 52, 3-4B** 3

Shoe Biz 877 Valencia St., (415) 550-8655, www.shoebizsf.com. From sneakers to trendy pink leather platform boots, this family-owned business has been selling shoes in San Francisco since 1979. This location, its newest, carries men's and women's footwear designed in Italy, Spain, and the US. The majority of the stock is hip casual wear at mid-range prices. Some of the brands include Vans, Tsubo and Irregular Choice. A wall of handbags by various designers, such as Onitsuka, add to the collection. **Map p. 52, 3B** 5

Skechers Footwear 2600 Mission St., (415) 401-6211, www.skechers.com. Skechers has become one of the top affordable sneaker and shoe brands for trendy mainstream fashion in recent years. Some of the brand's styles include high-impact cross-trainers, low-key slide shoes, fisherman sandals and flip-flops for men and women. For kids, there are Premium joggers and cross-band sandals. **Map p. 52, 4C** 8

Union Shoes Center 2118 Mission St., (415) 252-0138, www.unionshoe.com. Despite the store's appearance, which is a bit shabby looking and not all that inviting, the Union Shoes Center is worth a stop if you are looking for cheap shoes: most, even the leather shoes, are under $30. This is a good choice for families looking to save on kids' sneakers and shoes, as well. **Map p. 52, 3B** 13

CRAFTS & GIFTS

Atelier Posey et Susan 2720 16th St., (415) 776-6367. Functioning as both an art studio and shop, the Atelier is home to two Bay Area artists, sisters Posey and Susan Tibbon. Susan Tibbon is renowned for her hand-painted eggs, while Posey Tibbon has a following for her crocheted and lace designs. The two sell a few other items, such as hand-rolled beeswax candles and beautifully stitched pillows. The only drawback is the hours, which are limited. The Atelier is open 3.30 pm–5.30 pm on Fri and 11.30 am–5.30 pm on Saturday. Otherwise by appointment only. **Map p. 52, 4A** 🎴

Artist Xchange 3169 16th St., (415) 640-4725, www.artist-xchange.com. Owner Scott Mitchell runs this consignment gallery and stocks it with crafts and works by local artists. Nearly 85 artists are represented at any one time, through glassware, ceramics, sculpture, prints, paintings and jewellery. Though there are a few large pieces, most of the items are smaller and perfect for unique, artful gifts. Artist Xchange also holds occasional art fairs, where artists can sell direct. **Map p. 52, 3A-B** ⑪

Beadissimo 1051 Valencia St., (415) 282-2323, www.beadissimo.com. Creative types will find bliss at this bead shop where they can run their hands through beads and baubles of every shape, size, colour and material. Customers can either work on their bead projects at home or bring them into the store. The in-store experts can help and they also have beading, wire-working or stringing classes for beginning and more advanced hobbyists. **Map p. 52, 3C** ⑦

Brendan Lai's Supply Company 2075 Mission St., (415) 626-3314. Martial arts fans will find much to ogle at in this small, dingy shop. There are several glass cases displaying Yitin double-handed swords, metal kamas with steel blades, Wushu daggers and belts, daggers with sheaths, and more. The shop offers Kung Fu and Tai Chi books and magazines, posters of Bruce Lee and other film stars, Kung Fu action films, and martial arts T-shirts. **Map p. 52, 3B** ⑨

Encantada Gallery of Fine Art 904 Valencia St., (415) 642-3939. Encantada serves as both a gallery and arts and crafts shop, with a combination of fine quality gifts and complete kitsch. The shop carries lots of things of a Mexican or Chicano theme, including Frida Kahlo paraphernalia, Mexican wrestler masks, Mexican cookbooks, *nacimientos* (creche scenes), crosses and medals of saints. Many of the pieces in the store are imported directly from known Mexican artists and sold at good prices. **Map p. 52, 3B** ②

Botanica Yoruba 998 Valencia St., (415) 826-4967. Botanica Yoruba carries a wide variety of products from the Yoruba and Congo religions. Much of the merchandise comes from Cuba and Nigeria, and is geared toward people who practice Santeria, Lucumi, Ocha, Ifa and Las Reglas de Palo. The shop sells spiritual tools for ceremonies, including candles, dried herbs, incense, amulets, soperas, bateas, cauldrons and implements of the Orishas, or guardian spirits. Some of the services offered here include Spanish card readings, traditional caracoles readings and initiations. **Map p. 52, 3C** ❼

Hellenic American Imports 2365 Mission St., (415) 282-2237. The sign outside reads, 'My Big Fat Greek Import Store,' which aptly describes this shop. (The only deception is in the size of the store itself, which is narrow and small.) For some 40 years, this has been the place in San Francisco for those hard-to-find Greek wines, cheeses and pastries. It also sells large Grecian statues, painted vases, jewellery, Greek music and other curios. The owners pre-record a radio programme here for a local AM station. **Map p. 52, 3-4B** ❸

Casa Bonampak 3331 24th St., (415) 642-4079. Casa Bonampak specialises in Latin American folk art, clothing, cards, jewellery and other gift items. The store is filled with Day of the Dead pendants, Zapatista masks, flamenco postcards and a pretty full range of things with Che Guevara on them. Casa Bonampak's philosophy is to work directly with artisans from Oaxaca, Chiapas and Guatemala, and to promote fair trade with Latin America. **Map p. 52, 3C** ⓯

Currents 911 Valencia St., (415) 648-2200, www.currentssf.com. Currents makes its own line of bath and body herbs, herbal teas, massage oils, body salts and other holistic elixirs. The shop also carries other brands of bath and body items, such as natural vegetable soaps, aromatherapy candles, foot-care gift sets and lavender dream pillows. Much of the bath and body merchandise is labelled with the benefits of each herbal and natural blend. Also wool scarves, books on yoga, and recycled-paper notebooks. **Map p. 52, 3B** ❺

Good Vibrations 603 Valencia St., (415) 522-5460, www.goodvibes.com. A San Francisco classic. Opened in 1977 as a clean alternative to adult bookstores, this women-owned sex toy store has gained a respectful following in the Bay Area. Women and men alike can have fun browsing through the vibrators, bondage and fetish gear, body lotions and various erotica novelty items. There are numerous sex and porn DVDs to choose from, as well as a host of graphic novels and sex guidebooks. Good Vibrations also has a social conscience and does quite a bit of community outreach, including safe-sex workshops. **Map p. 52, 3B** ❷

Mission Gift Shop 2756 Mission St., (415) 824-3811. For those in search of Jesus statues, Jesus clocks, cross necklaces and other religious items, Mission Gift Shop is the place. Many items are imported from Europe and Asia. Some of the other gift items include Danea porcelain dolls, embroidered wall hangings, decorative tea sets and other housewares. **Map p. 52, 4C** ⓰

Ruby Gallery 3602 20th St., (877) 595-RUBY, www.rubygallery.com. Ruby Gallery is a San Francisco cooperative featuring jewellery and other art products, from housewares to fine art. Kathleen Maley makes her jewellery using sterling silver and vintage Czech, German and Japanese glass. The DAS label features handbags made of silk, suede, fake fur, and adorned with crystal beads as well as unusual corals and semi-precious beads. Other artists focus on glass works, candles, velvet-covered vases, and barrettes, to name a few items. **Map p. 52, 3B** 🟢

Studio 24 2857 24th St., (415) 826-8009. Operated by Galeria de la Raza, Studio 24 focuses on Mexican folk arts and crafts. The funky shop carries Oaxacan wood carvings, tin ornaments, Day of the Dead accoutrements, custom-made votive candles, pottery and art prints. There is also a line of artist-made T-shirts, colourful jewellery and books. Profits from the shop go toward support of the Galeria. **Off map**

Therapy 545 Valencia St., (415) 861-6213; 541 Valencia St., (415) 621-5902. Therapy's two locations both focus on retro-contemporary styles, but each store has a speciality. One features furniture, home furnishings, and small gift items, such as funky day-glo lamps, tiki shot glasses, and modern sofas and chairs that can be custom-upholstered. The second shop offers clothes, accessories and gift items, many having to do with drinking, such as cocktail swizzles and humorous shot glasses. Clothes and accessories are mostly Californian with some outside designers: names like Freepeople, Fossil and Paul Frank. **Map p. 52, 3B** 🔵

Thumbs Up Marbles 3422 25th St., (415) 920-8964, www.thumbsup marbles.com. Eclectic is the only appropriate word to describe Thumbs Up Marbles. The gift shop sells things like Betty Boop figures, Nepalese shawls, handmade pillow covers from India, colourful hanging mobiles, Frieda Kahlo lamps and quilts made by a Guatemalan women's cottage industry. There are a few religious items, such as crosses and Last Supper displays. The shop also sells marbles, as well as jewellery by local makers. **Map p. 52, 4D** 🔵

BOOKS

Adobe Bookshop 3166 16th St., (415) 864-3936. Adobe Bookshop looks more like someone's cluttered old basement than a bookshop, but it's an excellent spot for those who like a treasure hunt. Books are stacked in every nook and cranny, and on the floor. Though there are signs for genres (such as Western religion, gay and lesbian, history, etc.), there is no order to the inventory. Some titles may look a bit worse for the wear, but the prices are fair. The atmosphere here is very casual, with staff and customers sitting around on chairs, chatting or flipping through various titles. Adobe also has a small gallery showing up-and-coming Mission artists, and also offers readings and events. **Map p. 52, 3A-B** 11

Borderlands Books 866 Valencia St., (415) 824-8203, www.borderlands-books.com. This popular spot specialises in science fiction, fantasy and horror. The stock, both new and used, is neatly arranged and easy to look through. Borderlands also carries some rare and collectible titles, and has a section of horror and sci-fi DVDs. The bookstore holds author events on occasion and offers coffee and tea service in winter, when patrons can curl up with their books on the couches and chairs. **Map p. 52, 3B** 5

Dog Eared Books 900 Valencia St., (415) 282-1901, www.dogeared books.com. Dog Eared features some new titles, but about 70% of the stock is used. Most titles are fiction, including some remainders, where the customer benefits from an over-anticipation of demand by the publisher. Aside from fiction, Dog Eared carries political satire, a wide variety of art books and some comic books. The shop also sells new and used CDs, everything from punk and blues to imports from Cuba and Eastern Europe. **Map p. 52, 3B** 5

Forest Books 3080 16th St., (415) 863-2755. The selection at Forest Books resembles a private library belonging to someone with diverse tastes. All the stock is best-quality used, in such good condition they seem like new. More than half the stock is out-of-print books, many first editions. There is an emphasis on Asian culture and Eastern religions, with stock geared mainly toward the humanities. That said, there are still sections on fiction and children's books. Inside the glass cases are some of the signed collectibles. **Map p. 52, 3A-B** 7

La Casa del Libro 973 Valencia St., (415) 285-1399. All the titles in this general bookstore are Spanish-language. Topics cover the usual reference, fiction, history, and children's books. La Casa del Libro also carries Spanish-language magazines, as well as other small items such as Tarot cards. The shop regularly hosts author readings as well as book clubs and a theatre workshop for children. **Map p. 52, 3C** 19

Modern Times Bookstores 888 Valencia St., (415) 282-9246, www.mtbs.com. Opened as a collectively owned and operated bookstore in 1971, Modern Times has a wide range of titles, though it specialises in left-leaning culture and politics (one wall features pocket-sized Noam Chomsky books). The bookstore advertises itself as offering one of the Bay Area's most extensive collections of writings on Latino history and culture, in addition to its full selection of Spanish-language books. Books on sexuality and gender are also popular. Modern Times also sells magazines, independent 'zines, card sets and other small items. **Map p. 52, 3B** 5

Valencia Street Books 569 Valencia St., (415) 552-7200. The discriminating owner at Valencia Books describes her collection as 'books that don't suck'. Emphasis is on new books that are not easily found in mainstream shops. The soft, inviting chairs inside are an invitation to sit and get to know the titles. **Map p. 52, 3B** 17

MUSIC

Aquarius Records 1055 Valencia St., (415) 647-2272, www.aquarius records.org. This small music store has the distinction of being San Francisco's oldest independent record shop. Each title is staff-picked—they sift out what they consider rubbish, which means almost anything mainstream. Nearly every CD features a helpful description card with miniature reviews from various staff members. Though the shop is small, it is easy to spend hours sorting through the unique and offbeat titles. **Map p. 52, 3C** 7

Record Collector 3170 21st St., (415) 970-8400. This tiny shop off the main strip sells new and used LPs and 45s for the gamut of musical tastes. Vinyl collectors will also find some rare LPs here. The store also buys used records. Closed Monday and Sunday. **Map p. 52, 4C** 20

shop!

HOUSEWARES

Architectural Elements 573 Valencia St., (415) 252-8370, ae-home.com. Standing out among its Mission District peers, Architectural Elements is easily the neatest shop on the block. The home furnishings store carries cleanly designed modern furniture, with minimalist, colourful tendencies. Dutch, Italian, and American designers are all represented. Accessories are functional but have an elegant beauty, including beaded placemats, handmade ceramics, and brightly coloured glass from Mexico. **Map p. 52, 3B** 17

Den 849 Valencia St., (415) 282-6646, densf.com. Den owner Raymond Long tends toward classic modernist pieces in his furniture showroom, with an emphasis on form and function. Though Den carries a smattering of antiques, most of the stock is new. Long looks for one-of-a-kind and rare pieces from local designers and a handpicked few from around the country. He also showcases local vintage art as well as new works by Bay Area artists. The store is closed Mondays, unless it opens by appointment. **Map p. 52, 3B 5**

Designer Imports 2310 Mission St., (415) 285-2076. Spanning two floors, this inexpensive furniture shop is crammed to the hilt. Some of the pieces are in good shape, but it is a good idea to double-check the quality of each piece, as many items are cheaply made. **Map p. 52, 3-4B 3**

Don's Antiques 572 Valencia St., (415) 552-7616. Open Sat and Sun. One of the most entertaining proprietors on the block is Don Fried, a certified senior appraiser of antiques and decorative arts who only opens his doors on weekends. This is truly an antiques variety shop, each corner jammed with unique curiosities. Don's is known for the cases of costume jewellery organised by price. Also in stock are 18th-C to modern Chinese and Western paintings and prints, dollhouse furniture, vintage toys, desk sets, glassware, Victorian chairs, and paper memorabilia, such as old *Harpers Weekly* magazines and vintage postcards. **Map p. 52, 3B 17**

The Furniture Center 2301 Mission St., (415) 970-0312. The Furniture Center stands out among the dizzying array of discount furniture shops along Mission Street. The quality here is better than at many others, while the prices are still reasonable. The lower floor is filled with large sofas, chaises longue and chairs, though it is not as crammed as some of the other stores. **Map p. 52, 3-4C 21**

Harrington Bros. 599 Valencia, (415) 861-7300, harringtonbros.com. Anyone who enjoys a good flea market or garage sale will enjoy sorting through this showroom full of antiques and collectibles. Some of the goods are in top condition, including some of the wood furniture and china cabinets. There is a lot of that some would label junk here, such as the numerous run-down rocking chairs. A few assorted items such as an old cash register and pinball machine would appeal to collectors. **Map p. 52, 3B 2**

Paxton Gate 824 Valencia St., (415) 824-1872. Loosely labelled a garden shop, Paxton Gate offers much more than flower shears and potting soil. Shopping at Paxton is like a class on entomology, and the store holds the distinction of having the widest variety of stuffed beasts in the city. The curiosities here include a butterfly collection, dead beetles, stuffed armadillos, Trilobite fossils and an articulated monkey skeleton. For the brave, Paxton sells boxes of chocolate-covered insects. **Map p. 52, 3B 6**

Rayon Vert 3187 16th St., (415) 861-3516. Aside from its impeccable seasonal and floral displays, Rayon Vert can spruce up any home with its furnishings and gift items. Owner Kelly Kornegay sets up the smaller items—candles, vintage maps, beach glass, stationery, bath products and books—on and around the furniture she sells. Closed Sunday and Monday. **Map p. 52, 3A-B** 11

The Touch 956 Valencia St., (415) 550-2640, www.thetouch.us. One of the more chic home furnishing outlets in the area, the Touch specialises in quality used pieces. The store prides itself on its extensive collection of armoires from England and France, and other vintage gear includes Art Deco, Mid-Century, and Danish Modern designs. Its Swarovski chandelier selection, featuring more than 40 styles, is renowned. There are a few interesting extras sitting about, such as a velvet Elvis and vintage typewriters. **Map p. 52, 3C** 19

Valencia Interiors 974 Valencia St., (415) 647-9500, www.valenciainteriors. com. Add Valencia Interiors to the long list of furniture shops along Valencia Street. The stock here for the most part is new, though the shop carries a few second-hand pieces. Pieces come from all over the world. The attraction here is craftsmanship at decent prices. **Map p. 52, 3C** 19

X-21 Modern 890 Valencia St., (415) 647-4211, www.x21modern.com. While X-21 specialises in vintage office furniture, mainly 1950s–1970s, it's the store's other obsession that gets all the attention: X-21's owners have a fondness for oversized items. A giant bagel, watch, soda bottle and various politician heads hang for your amusement. The store also carries chairs shaped like hands and downstairs there is a massive basement crammed with lamps, chairs, desks, everything stacked in disarray. **Map p. 52, 3B** 5

Z-Barn 560 Valencia St., (415) 864-5800, www.z-barn.com. The elegant interior of this shop is carefully decorated with handcrafted furniture from around the world. Z-Barn is known for its solid, hardwood furnishings from India, Romania, China, Indonesia, Morocco and Vietnam, as well as sofas from local designers. The furniture is all new, but not marked up as much as in other shops. There are also knick-knacks for sale, as well as children's books. Closed Wednesday. **Map p. 52, 3B** 17

HAYES VALLEY &
CIVIC CENTER

The Asian Art Museum

CHONG-MOON LEE CENTER FOR ASIAN ART AND CULTURE

OPEN	10 am–5 pm, Tue–Sun; until 9 pm on Thur
CHARGES	$10 adults; $7 seniors; $6 ages 12–17; free for children under 12. $5 on Thur after 5 pm; free first Tuesday of the month. Free with City Pass and Go San Francisco cards.
GUIDED VISITS	Free audio tours available from the information desk on the ground floor. Docent tours offered throughout the day.
DISABLED ACCESS	From main entrance. All rooms are wheelchair-accessible; wheelchairs and folding stools available at coat check.
SERVICES	Museum store, Café Asia on ground floor
TELEPHONE	(415) 581-3500
WEB	www.asianart.org
MAIN ENTRANCE	200 Larkin St., between McAllister and Grove. Parking available across the street at the underground Civic Center Garage.
GETTING THERE	Take BART or Muni to Civic Center Station

HIGHLIGHTS

The Bodhisattva Maitreya	Gallery 1
Bridle cheekpieces from Luristan	Gallery 7
Decorated box of Maharaja Ranjit Singh	Gallery 6
Jade collection	Gallery 13
Chinese bronze vessels	Gallery 14
Chinese Money Tree	Gallery 15
Seated Buddha	Gallery 16
Goryeo Celadon Pottery	Gallery 21
Brahma (Japanese Bonten) and Indra (Japanese Taishakuten)	Gallery 26
Collection of Netsuke and Inro	Gallery 27
Traditional Teahouse	Gallery 30
Bamboo Baskets from the Cotsen Collection	Gallery 30

ASIAN ART MUSEUM

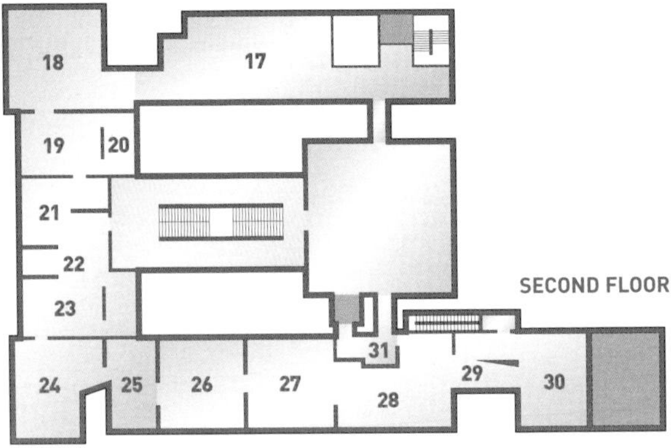

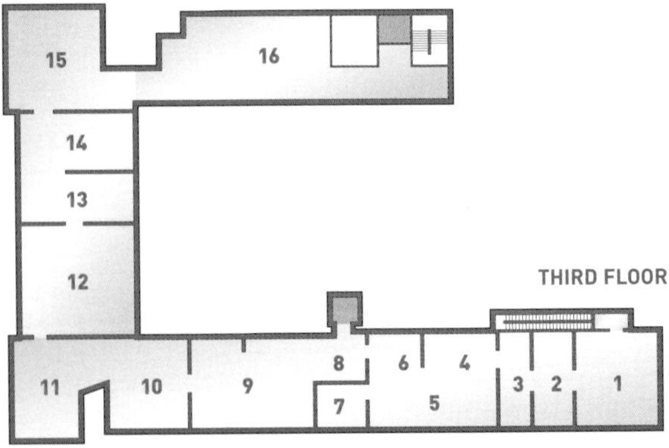

18 17

19 20

21

22

23

24 25 26 27 28 31 29 30

SECOND FLOOR

15 16

14

13

12

11 10 9 8 6 4 3 2 1
7 5

THIRD FLOOR

The Asian Art Museum was established in 1966 when Chicago industrialist Avery Brundage donated his considerable collection to the city of San Francisco. For 35 years the museum shared a building with the de Young Museum in Golden Gate Park, before moving to its present location on Civic Center Plaza in 2003. The first American museum to focus exclusively on the arts of Asia, the permanent collection includes more than 15,000 pieces of art, one of the most comprehensive collections of Asian art in the world. In addition to nearly 40,000 square feet of gallery display space, through its AsiaAlive programme the museum hosts a series of live performances, hands-on activities and artist demonstrations aimed at fostering the understanding of Asian cultures.

THE BUILDING

The Asian Art Museum is part of the Civic Center complex, one of the most complete collections of beaux-arts buildings in America. Originally built in 1917 to house the San Francisco Main Library, the building was remodelled under the direction of museum designer Gae Aulenti, who also designed the Musée d'Orsay in Paris. Aulenti combined the traditional and the modern by retaining the beaux-arts façade and central core of the museum, while creating a sky-lit court on the ground floor and bridges that connect the galleries to the refurbished Samsung Hall. While the galleries are accessed via elevators or a two-level escalator, make sure to walk up the grand staircase, which ascends beneath a series of inspirational library inscriptions.

THE COLLECTION

The Asian Art Museum is arranged on three floors, with the special exhibition galleries on the first floor. Though it is possible to wander in and out of galleries at will, the collection was designed to be viewed in order, starting on the third floor. To begin, ascend the lift from the South Court (or take the elevator nearby) to the third floor. The galleries are arranged chronologically by region, with Chinese art split between the second and third floor.

SOUTH ASIA

Gallery 1 covers **SOUTH ASIA UNTIL 600**. Here you'll find a series of sculptures of early fertility gods and Buddhas. Starting at the left of the entrance, you can note the change from the somewhat simplistic style of the early Buddhas to the more elaborate **Bodhisattva Maitreya** (c. 100–300 BC), carved from dark grey schist. The two Bodhisattva figures here show Greco-Roman influences, attesting to the influence of the colonies established by Alexander the Great after he conquered Persia in 330 BC.

In *Gallery 2* is **EASTERN INDIAN ART FROM 600–1600**. On either side of the entrance are a series of Hindu and Buddhist sculptures, set in niches in the wall in an attempt to replicate the manner in which they would have been displayed in a traditional temple. Both Buddhism and Hinduism flourished at this time, and a single workshop might have produced statues for either religion.

For a good example of differences in Indian regional art styles, look at the three **Vishnu sculptures** on the far side of the room, to the right of the doorway. The materials available in each region had a great impact on how the art style developed. The far right figure comes from Southern India and is carved in schist, with elaborate details. The centre figure comes from North Central India and is carved in sandstone, which is unable to support detailed carvings. To the left is a Vishnu sculpture from East India carved in pyllite, which accommodates moderate detailing.

Gallery 3 showcases **ART FROM CENTRAL AND WESTERN INDIA, 600-1600**. The left side of the gallery is devoted to the sculptures and art of Jainism, a religion that stressed meditation, self-denial and nonviolence. Jainism was based on teachings of twenty-four leaders, shown here in the bronze *Twenty-four Jain Teachers* (1493). Note also the white marble temple decorations, *Female Celestial Holding a Fly Whisk and Water Pot*, and *Female Celestial Playing a Drum* (c. 1100–1300), displayed high on the wall. The round faces and large eyes are common in Jain art.

Gallery 4 features **ART FROM SOUTH INDIA, 600–1600**. It's interesting to compare the elaborate *Ganesha* (1400–1600), holding a piece of his own trunk, with the first simple Gahesha sculptures at the start of the galleries. The bronze Ganesha is surrounded by an arched horseshoe halo, the metal allowing for a freestanding sculpture with fanciful decorations.

With *Gallery 5*, **SOUTH ASIA AFTER 1600**, we begin to see influences from the outside world—China, Portugal and England. The blue and white porcelain *Chinese Plate with Grape Design from Jiangxi Province* (1426–1435) belonged to a Mughal emperor in India, while the lead glass *Base for a Water Pipe* (1690–1700) was manufactured in England for sale in India, designed to satisfy a new demand for the tobacco introduced by Portuguese traders.

Before the British were the Mughals (1526–1858); at the height of their power, this Indo-Islamic dynasty ruled a good portion of present day Pakistan, Afghanistan and India. **Mughals jade** is famous, and a number of pieces can be seen here. Note the jade *Cup with 19th-C French Fittings* (1650–1750).

THE PERSIAN WORLD AND WEST ASIA

Continuing straight you'll find yourself in *Gallery 7*, **THE PERSIAN WORLD AND WESTERN ASIA**. This small room contains some of the oldest pieces in the museum, such as the **earthenware vessels** (1000–800 BC) and the *Footed Bowl* (4000–3000 BC) decorated with stylised images of wild goats. This piece is from Tepe Sialk, a site in modern-day Iran that was excavated in the 1930s. The following *Bronze Bridle Cheekpieces* (1000–650 BC) reflect the nomadic lifestyle of the people of the Luristan region.

After the Mongol invasion of Persia in 1200, trade was revived between Central Asia and China. The pottery on the far wall shows Chinese influences in various pieces.

Gallery 6 features **pieces from the Sikh Kingdom** of Northern India. The *Decorated Box* owned by Maharaja Ranjit Singh (c. 1660–1700) inlaid with ivory and tortoiseshell and decorated with ivory panels shows the delicacy of workmanship and style of the Sikh court.

SOUTHEAST ASIA

With *Gallery 8*, the focus moves to Southeast Asia—Burma (Myanmar), Thailand, Laos, Cambodia, Vietnam, Malaysia, Singapore, Indonesia, Brunei and the Philippines. The pieces here demonstrate to the casual viewer how Hinduism and Buddhism flourished and Sanskrit was adopted as the language of the court. Note the Buddha figures, such as a *Head of Buddha* (650–850), from Draravati, an early Thai culture. In *Gallery 9*, which deals with **SOUTHEAST ASIA IN THE PERIOD 600–1300**, is art from the Angkor Kingdom of Cambodia.

When leaving *Gallery 9*, notice the sandstone *Lintel* (approx. 975–1025) hung over the doorway. It is typical of the decorative carvings found on Buddhist and Hindu temples in the Angkor kingdom; faces of monsters and deities protected the temples and visitors.

Gallery 10, which shows **ART FROM 1300–1800**, highlights the great changes that occurred in Southeast Asia at this time. The Kingdom of Angkor lost power and Mahayana Buddhism and Hinduism were given up in all but a few places, though Theravada Buddhism continued to flourish. Islam won converts in Malaysia and the Spanish brought Christianity to the Philippines. In Thailand, the **Kingdoms of Sukhotai and Ayutthaya** grew strong. The *Head of the Buddha* (1350–1450) is an example of Sukhotai art; the elongated grace of this Buddha is distinctly Thai. On the left wall, the *Reclining Buddha* (1600–1700) shows the Buddha dying, one of four positions in which he is traditionally portrayed. In Thailand, there are similar Buddhas that measure up to 92 feet.

The following hallway is lined with examples of the **kris**, a Malay Indonesian dagger, many of which have ornate handles. Make sure to take a look at the elaborate Kris holder in the form of a demon (1800–1900).

Gallery 11, South East Asia after 1800, begins with a colourful display of **Indonesian rod puppets**. The centrepiece of this room is the *Crowned and Bejewelled Buddha Image and Throne* (1850–1900), from a 19th-C Burmese temple. On either side are two Thai *Buddhas Dressed in Royal Garb* (1850–1900), commissioned by Thai kings to commemorate deceased royal relatives. As you leave this gallery, notice the lovely *Palace Door* (1800–1900). The phoenix and the peony flowers are images imported from Chinese art.

THE HIMALAYAS AND THE TIBETAN BUDDHIST WORLD
In *Gallery 12*, **HIMALAYAN AND TIBETAN BUDDHIST ART** is displayed. Buddhism was introduced in the early 600s from

India and China, but evolved into a unique and distinct religion with a strong emphasis on monastic life. Tibetan Buddhism pays homage to a large number of deities; the *White Tara* (1400–1500) is just one (the shiny golden surface of this figure is achieved through a mercury gilding process). The nearby *Buddhist Deity Simhavaktia Dakini* (1736–1795) is another deity from Tibetan Buddhism, although it is a Qing Dynasty sculpture from China. It shows Tibetan Buddhism's impact on its neighbour to the north, where the Mongol emperor Khubilai Khan (1215–1294) converted to Tibetan Buddhism and made it the state religion.

Make sure to visit the rotating display of **Thangka paintings** of deities or mandalas displayed in this room.

CHINA

Gallery 13 offers a truly overwhelming display of **Chinese jade**, a stone that has long held ritual significance in China. The *Openwork Incense Box* (1900–1945) is a delightful example of the delicacy of carving that can be achieved with this prized stone.

The **ART OF CHINA TO 221 BC** is displayed in *Gallery 14*. The long legs on many of the bronze vessels, such as the *Shang Dynasty Ritual Wine Vessel*, the so-called Yayi Jia, (1300–1050 BC), from Henan Province, allowed them to be placed over a fire.

The Shang Dynasty fell in 1050 BC to the Zhou, who ruled over a feudal system beset by uncertainty and violence. In 220 BC the Qin triumphed and united the country. During this time trade increased and technological advancements such as the use of iron led to greater wealth.

In *Gallery 15*, **CHINA FROM 221 BC TO 960 AD**, you will find the striking *Money Tree* (25–220 AD), which illustrates not only the Chinese practice of ancestor worship but also the growing importance of Buddhism. The earthenware base of the Money Tree symbolises life on earth. From the earth, the soul was thought to travel up six levels—designated by the six levels of branches hung with coins—to the paradise of the Queen Mother of the West. Note the small Buddha in the tree, as well as the deity busy preparing a magic elixir from the lingzhi fungus, a symbol of longevity.

The porcelain that China would grow famous for began to be produced in the mid-500s AD in northern China. The first products were entirely white, such as the *Dish with Incised Lotus Design* (900–1000).

Gallery 16 is devoted to **CHINESE BUDDHIST ART**. At the beginning of the gallery you will see one of the treasures of the museum, the *Seated Buddha* (338), the earliest accurately dated Chinese Buddha. It is modelled on the Buddha figures from northern India, but Chinese modifications can be seen in the thick robes, childlike expression and almond eyes. The gallery that follows shows a variety of Buddhist sculptures and stelae. Though Buddhism had flourished in the early Tang Dynasty, in 845 Emperor Wu—acting on the advice of Taoist and Confucian advisers—began to persecute Buddhists. This period saw the destruction of 4,600 Buddhist monasteries and their artwork.

The second floor begins with a collection of **Chinese porcelain** housewares and domestic objects that illustrate Chinese good luck symbols. These images appear on a number of objects in *Gallery 17*, which covers **CHINA 960–1911**.

The **Ming Dynasty** (1368–1644) saw a concerted effort to revive ethnic Chinese culture, after the rule of the foreign Yuan Emperors. Ming Emperors commissioned ceramics and the entire court supported the arts. The *Covered Jar Decorated with Lotus Pond* (1368–1644) is a lovely example of Ming porcelain.

Song and Ming emperors valued **ancient Chinese bronzes** for the link they provided with the great emperors of old, and commissioned works in the same style. You'll notice the similarities between these new bronzes and the originals in *Gallery 14*. The scholarly arts are also represented here, with a display of **scholar's equipment** from the Ming and early Qing Dynasties: candlesticks, ink stands, brush box. As you leave this gallery, take a look at the *Emperor's Semiformal Court Robe* (1800–1900). Worn by a Qing Emperor, this intricately embroidered robe contains a series of auspicious symbols as well as the nine heavenly dragons that could be worn only by an emperor.

Gallery 18 showcases **CHINESE PAINTING** on paper and silk. In order to protect the paintings, this gallery rotates its collection on

Seated Buddha *(dated 338)* China, Latter Zhao dynasty

a regular basis. Chinese painting from the late 1500s onward falls into one of two categories: paintings by court artists and paintings completed for the educated elite. The court paintings tend towards bright colours and bold brushwork, and were used to decorate palaces and temples. Paintings for the elite had a limited colour palette and were for private viewing.

In *Gallery 19*, **CHINESE IMPERIAL ARTS 1644–1911**, a *Qing Dynasty Throne* (1800–1880) is set before a lacquered screen depicting *Prosperity in an Imperial Palace* (1670), one of the earliest examples of this type of screen. To the far side of the room is a display that recreates a section of wall in the Shugangzhai ('Hall of Floating Fragrance') in the Imperial Compound. Also note the stunningly embroidered *Bed Cover* (1800–1900).

To the left of this gallery is *Gallery 20*, dedicated to **Chao Shao-an**, a leading painter in the Lingnan movement, which began to integrate western artistic techniques into Chinese painting.

KOREA

With *Gallery 21*, the focus turns to **EARLY KOREAN ART THROUGH 1392**. A series of **earthenware vessels from the Three Kingdoms Period** (57 BC–668 AD) are displayed on the right. Buddhism was introduced from China to Korea and by the mid 500s had been adopted by all three of the Korean kingdoms. The **Silla stoneware urns** you'll see displayed here were used to hold ashes. The Silla Kingdom unified Korea in 668, and the figures, such as the *Standing Buddha* (700–800) dates from the Unified Silla Dynasty, which was succeeded by the Goryeo Dynasty (918–1392). There was a strong demand for Buddhist art by the Goryeo court, and the Goryeo were also responsible for some of the finest celadon porcelain.

In the following Joseon Dynasty (1392–1910), pottery styles continued to evolve, as can be seen in the three freestanding displays in this gallery. The all-white style led to the blue and white of the *Jar with Tiger and Magpie* (1800–1900). This fell out of favour, replaced by iron oxide decoration, such as on *Jar with Dragon Decoration* (1600–1675).

The adjoining *Gallery 23* shows **WORKS FROM KOREA FROM 1392 TO THE PRESENT**.

JAPAN

The early Japanese pieces date from **the Jomon period** (8000–300 BC). The earthenware vessels here are mainly simple pots decorated with the cord design that gives the Jomon period its name. The **Yayoi pottery** (300 BC–300 AD), though still made by coil, is smoother and more symmetrical.

Gallery 26 shows **JAPANESE BUDDHIST ART**. Buddhism took root in Japan when the Korean king sent a gift to the Japanese emperor that included a statue of Buddha as well as sacred Buddhist texts and other ritual objects. After a brief struggle between supporters of Buddhism and the Shinto religion, Buddhism was chosen by the Japanese court and widely adopted. One of the treasures in this gallery is the *Standing Brahma* (Japanese Boten) and *Indra* (Japanese Taisha Kuten), which date from 710–800 and were made for one of the most important temples in Nara, Kofukuji. Made by dry lacquer technique, an expensive and time-consuming process, they are the only examples of the type in the US.

In *Gallery 27*, **JAPANESE ARTS OF DAILY LIFE FROM THE END OF 1100s TO THE MID-1800s**, you can trace the rise of the samurai culture. The *Suit of Armour* (1615–1868), *Campaign Coat* (1800s) and *Stirrups* (1615–1868) all speak to the power of the samurai during this time. Also notable is the large collection of **netsuke and inro** on display in this gallery. These playful miniature sculptures were popular from the 1500s to the mid-1800s, and portray themes from Japanese literature, folktales, history and theatre.

Gallery 28 features **Japanese paintings and screens** and Japanese porcelain. Note the regional style differences, from the white Nabeshima ware, with decorations of blue, green, yellow and red, to the Ko Kutani with brighter, bolder designs in blue, green and yellow.

Gallery 29 has Japanese **porcelain and prints of the Edo period** (1615–1868). The life of the newly emerging urban middle class is depicted in these prints of teahouses, brothels and theatres.

Tea drinking was brought to Japan from China around 1200 and *Gallery 30* explores tea-related arts. The tea bowls and other ceramics displayed here show the Wabicha preference for a rustic aesthetic, which is also reflected in the display of **modern Japanese pottery**, with ceramics from the Folk Art Movement of the 1920s.

The far case in this gallery displays a selection from the museum's collection of 800 **bamboo baskets**. A typical teahouse is reconstructed in this gallery as well—make sure to go around to the far end, where you can see into the tea preparation room (*mizuya*) at the rear.

Though you can reach the exit from this gallery, make sure to backtrack into *Gallery 28* and then take the bridge to Samsung Hall. With *Gallery 31* and the Betty Bogart Contemplative Alcove, Izumi Masatoshi's *Tsukubai* (Basin) takes us into contemporary Japanese art. A protégée of Isamu Noguchi, Masatoshi has created an interplay with stone and water that translates traditional Japanese aesthetics into the modern.

in the area

Alamo Square This square presents a quintessential San Francisco tableau: a block of elegant Victorians in the foreground, with the skyscrapers of the Financial District rising behind them. No wonder these houses on Steiner Street, between Grove and Hayes, are known as 'postcard row'. Not only are they endlessly photographed, but they have also appeared repeatedly in film and on television. When they were built in the 1890s, one of these homes would have fetched $4,000. Today the price tag exceeds $1 million. **Map p. 76, 1B**

Haas-Lilienthal House 2007 Franklin St. (between Washington and Jackson), (415) 441-3000. Open 12 pm–3 pm, Wed and Sat; 11 am–4 pm, Sun. Guided tours only $8/$5. A tour of this splendid Queen Anne Victorian house provides a rare window on the lifestyle of the city's 19th-C elite. Built in 1886, it was home to a

Alamo Square

German-Jewish family in the grocery trade. Almost all the furniture and fittings are original (including trompe-l'oeil wood panelling). Features such as the servants' quarters speak volumes about the conventions of the time. Take the #1, 12, 19, 27, 47 or 49 bus or the California Street cable car to the end of the line at California and Van Ness. **Off map**

City Hall 1 Dr. Carlton B. Goodlett Place, (415) 554-6023. Open 8 am–8 pm, Tue–Fri; 12 pm–4 pm, Sat. Free 45-minute guided tours at 10 am, 12 pm and 2 pm, Mon–Fri; 12.30 pm Sat. Architecturally, San Francisco has always relied heavily on influences from elsewhere. For City Hall, the inspiration comes all the way from absolutist France. The dazzling dome was based on that of Les Invalides, commissioned by Louis XIV (indeed, cameos of the Sun King adorn City Hall's arches). But envy did not stop there: this gilded palace was pointedly built 16 feet taller than the US Capitol building in Washington DC. The result is that municipal government has never looked more regal. City Hall is the crown of the Civic Center, an architectural ensemble whose harmony epitomises the turn-of-the-20th-C 'City Beautiful' movement. From Fisherman's Wharf, take bus #47 or 49 down Van Ness Ave.; from Union Square, take the F streetcar west to 10th St. **Map p. 76, 4B**

eat

$ **Moishe's Pippic** 25/A Hayes St. (at Gough), (415) 431-2440 San Francisco suffers from a lack of good Jewish delis, but Moishe's is an exception to this rule. Because it's a true-hearted Chicago deli, Reubens and pastrami sandwiches are not the only reason to go there—the hot dogs are a major attraction. Don't think of anemic little floppy things, these are serious food. **Map p. 76, 4B** ❶

Tommy's Joynt 1101 Geary Blvd., (415) 775-4216, www.tommys joynt.com. Open 11 am-1.45 pm daily. If you've ever lost anything, you might well find it here. The walls—and floor!— of this spacious survivor of the 1906 earthquake are covered in all sorts of paraphernalia, memorabilia, knick-knacks and bric-a-brac. In addition to a long bar with a huge selection of beers from around the world, the house speciality is buffalo stew and buffalo chilli. For dessert try their famous cheesecake. You'll recognise the restaurant immediately for the swirling, colourful painted exterior. **Map p. 76, 3A** ❷

$$ **Indigo** 687 McAllister St., (415) 673-9353. Dinner: 5 pm–9.30 pm, Tue–Thur; until 11 pm, Fri and Sat; until 9.30 pm, Sun. Simple, clean lines bring a touch of Manhattan industrial sophistication combined with California comfortable elegance to Indigo, which has garnered a good response for its affordable 'New American' menu (think grilled chicken breast over roasted potatoes, ravioli filled with sweet potato and spinach, and, of course, steak). There's a prix fixe from 5 pm–7 pm and the Ultimate Wine Dinner from 8 pm. **Map p. 76, 3A-B** ❸

Max's Opera Café 601 Van Ness Ave., (415) 771-7300, www.maxs world.com. Open 11.30 am–10 pm, Mon; until 11 pm, Tue–Thur and Sun; until 2 am on Fri; until 1 am on Sat. Ah, the genre of the 'aria restaurant', where waiters double as tenors and the busboy sings bass. Max's is a large yet cosy place, with wide picture windows looking out on busy Van Ness. It's part of a local deli chain, but at heart it sticks to its New York roots. **Map p. 76, 3A** ❹

Paul K 199 Gough St. (at Oak), (415) 552-7132. Open 5 pm–10 pm, Tues–Thur; until 11 pm, Fri and Sat; until 9.30 pm, Sun. Paul K defines itself as 'edgy', which seems to mean art on the walls, an open kitchen and a menu with creative interpretations of eastern Mediterranean food. The space is dark and intimate and modern, and the proximity of Paul K to the theatres and opera means it's a popular place for a good pre-show meal. It's particularly appreciated among locals for the appetisers. **Map p. 76, 3B** ❺

Zuni Café 1658 Market St., (415) 552-2522. Open 11.30 am–12 am, Tue–Sat; 11 am–11 pm, Sun. In a way, Zuni *is* San Francisco. California comfort food like roast chicken and Chardonnay, wide plate glass windows to let in the light, and an copper-panelled atmosphere that encourages relaxation seem to typify the California experience. That might be the secret to Zuni's longevity; it's been around for more than 20 years, a real success story in a city with a constantly changing restaurant landscape. **Map p. 76, 3B** ❻

$$$$ **Jardinière** 300 Grove St. (at Franklin), (415) 861-5580. Open 5 pm–10.30 pm, Sun–Wed, until 11.30 pm, Thur–Sat. Hours are extended to accommodate performances at the nearby theatres and opera house. Jardinière is one of San Francisco's limelight restaurants, with its interior by famed maker of restaurant design magic Pat Kuleto (he also did ocean-themed Farallon, see p. 33). Chef Traci Des Jardins is committed to organics, and a seasonally changing menu means always fresh ingredients for the California French dishes. The dramatically elegant yet comfortable interior has an appealing, old-fashioned opulence. **Map p. 76, 3B** **7**

shop

CLOTHES

Azalea Boutique 411 Hayes St., (415) 861–9888, www.azaleasf.com. Azalea owners and designers Catherine Chow and Corina Nurimba traverse the globe in search of independent fashions that buck the mass-production trend. Some of the designers include Australia's Sass & Bide, Montreal's Kitchen Orange, Adriano Goldschmied Jeans and Second. Azalea also offers its own private label, as well as shoes from London's Beatrice Ong. Men will find designs from Ted Baker, J. Lindeberg, and James Perse. The boutique also features a nail bar salon, dubbed the Z Beauty Lounge, that steers clear of chemical products in favour of natural nail treatments. Pedicures include a peppermint and lavender soak, and all polishes are formaldehyde free. **Map p. 76, 3B** **1**

Cop. Copine 350 Hayes St., (415) 252-7719. Parisian women's clothing boutique Cop. Copine adds another touch of sophistication to the area. Cop. Copine is renowned for its chic, yet slightly offbeat fashions for women, even those who may not fit into a petite twenty-something waist. The shop also carries the Uko label, another San Francisco favourite. Prices are surprisingly affordable. **Map p. 76, 3B** **2**

Coulars 327 Hayes St., (415) 255-2925. Chic styles with an artistic flair fill this small Hayes Valley boutique. The catalyst for this shop's colourful touch is its owner, Dutch-born Marijke Coulars, who many years ago made hand-painted clothes. Now Coulars hand-picks the clothes she stocks. Most of the pieces are separates that Coulars will help customers coordinate into classy sets. **Map p. 76, 3B** ❷

Dark Garden 321 Linden St., (415) 431-7684, www.darkgarden.com. Anyone with a corset fetish will feel at home at Dark Garden. Corsets are handmade in a variety of fabrics, including satin, brocade, silk jacquard and leather. While most styles are for women, Dark Garden carries corsets for men, too. Historical costumes as well as circus outfits can be made, but the handcrafted corsets take six to eight weeks to complete. One-of-a-kind, handmade wedding dresses are also a speciality of the house, and require two to three months of work. **Map p. 76, 3B** ❶

Dish 541 Hayes St., (415) 252-5997. A Berkeley institution recently expanded to San Francisco. This women's clothing boutique features well-known as well as up-and-coming designers, mostly from New York and LA. Names include Theory, Beth Bowley, BCBG, Tina Turk, Lauren Moffat and Rebecca Taylor. Accessories are also a Dish speciality. **Map p. 76, 3B** ❸

Haseena 526 Hayes St., (415) 252-1104. Haseena's stock has a decidedly feminine flavour that runs through everything from slim-cut dresses to sultry lingerie. Focusing on women's clothes, Haseena places burgeoning local designers alongside larger name brands. Labels here include Parallel, Sunhee Moon and Mary Green. Expect moderate to high prices. **Map p. 76, 3B** ❸

Lava9 542 Hayes St., (415) 552-6468. Leather is the material of choice at Lava9. Store owner Heidi Weiner designs premium designer leather jackets in men's, women's and children's sizes and can custom-fit jackets as well. Some of the leather handbags in Lava9 are also her creations. **Map p. 76, 3B** ❸

MAC 387 Grove St., (415) 863-3011. MAC, which stands for Modern Apparel Clothing, fills its large space with chic men's and women's fashions, most often by progressive designers from Belgium. Check the details—each piece of clothing boasts fine stitching and design. MAC carries local labels, as well, but clothing isn't the only art form at MAC; the store fills its space with funky artistic works, including sculptures scattered about the floor. **Map p. 76, 3B** ❹

Manifesto 514 Octavia St., (415) 431-4778. The men's and women's clothes at Manifesto are created by designers and store owners Sarah Franko and Suzanne Castillo, who until a few years ago used to design the clothes on site. Now the duo has a separate design space, while the boutique shows off the Manifesto line of vintage designs. The 1940s- and 1950s-style dresses, blouses, suits and coats use rayon. Closed Monday and Tuesday. **Map p. 76, 3B**

Minnie Wilde 519 Laguna St., (415) 863-9453, www.minniewilde.com. Minnie Wilde is a hip design label based at this Hayes Valley boutique. Owners Terri Olson and Ann D'Apice launched their business literally in their garage, but have since become one of the city's trendiest design teams. The duo focuses on edgy, retro wear for women, hearkening back to the 1960s and 1970s. Their emphasis is on casual comfort, with a bit of pizzazz. Minnie Wilde also sells belts, mini trench coats and printed tees. **Map p. 76, 2B**

Nida 544 Hayes St., 552-4670; 564 Hayes St., (415) 552-4671. Nida opened its Hayes Valley location in March 2001 as a sister to its more established Union Street locale. The Hayes shop features designers mostly from Europe, and a few Americans: Helmut Lang, Costume National, Citizens of Humanity, Marc Jacobs and Vanessa Bruno. Skylights help illuminate the stripped down, modern interior. Nida has also opened a third Hayes Valley store focusing on trendy clothes for twenty-somethings. **Map p. 76, 3B**

Nomads 556 Hayes St., (415) 864-5692. This long-time San Francisco fashion spot caters mainly to men with its upscale line and looks mostly to Europe for its designers. Some of the labels featured include Fred Perry and Ben Sherman, as well as jeans by OneTrueSaxon and Von Dutch. Nomads does carry some local designers, such as Hank Ford and Lat Naylor, as well as a selection of vintage leather jackets. **Map p. 76, 3B**

She 501 Fell St., (415) 552-4030. Never mind the store's name, both men and women will find chic, trendy styles at She. The women's clothing designers include Anna Huling, Blithe and Kenzi, while men's wear is created by the likes of Custo, Toku and Dolce Leche. While the clothes are casual, they are sassy enough for a Saturday night out at the clubs. The boutique-level prices are actually reasonable for this neighbourhood. **Map p. 76, 2B**

Smaak 528 Hayes St., (415) 503-1430. Anyone partial to bright, loud colours will find a potential closet full of clothes at Smaak (it means 'taste'). The boutique maintains a narrow focus, stocking men's and women's fashions made in Scandinavia. Many of the styles are basic, some are quirky, while others tend toward the sleek. Designers include Twist & Tango and Filippa K. **Map p. 76, 3B**

RAG—Residents Apparel Gallery 541 Octavia St., (415) 621-7718. More of a collective than a shop, RAG features the designs of more than twenty Bay Area clothing artists, focusing mostly on women's apparel. Though some designers are originally from overseas, the catch is that each must currently live in the Bay Area. Designers rent space in the gallery to present their work. Many of the designs can only be found at RAG. **Map p. 76, 3B** ❺

Ver Unica 437B Hayes St., (415) 431-0688, www.ver-unica.com. Dubbing itself a 'fashion-forward vintage boutique', Ver Unica carries only the finest vintage stock. Clothes span the early 20th C as far as the 1980s. The shop is also known for its vintage accessories such as designer handbags and shoes. Some of the pieces in the store have never been worn. **Map p. 76, 3B** ❶

Zeni 567 Hayes St., (415) 864-0154. Nobody feels left out at Zeni, which brings together professional and casual fashions for men and women. Young fashionites can fork out hundreds of dollars for a designer leather jacket or just a fraction of that for a basic top. Designers include Kenzo, Diane Von Furstenburg, Anna Sui, Easel and Max Azria. Aside from outside labels, Zeni creates its own line of apparel, and carries designer accessories. Clothes can be altered. **Map p. 76, 3B** ❸

SHOES

Bulo Shoes Women's: 418 Hayes St., (415) 255-4939. Men's: 437A Hayes St., (415) 864-3244, www.buloshoes.com. The majority of Bulo Women's casual and dress shoes carry an Italian label. Some of the brands include Graffia, Alberto Fermani, Cydwoq, Sciapo and Mauro Giuli. High-quality leather and suede handbags in a variety of colours and sizes are also a Bulo main attraction. **Map p. 76, 3B** ❶

Gimme Shoes 416 Hayes St., (415) 864-0691, www.gimmeshoes.com. The line-up of designers at this small San Francisco chain is impressive. Emphasising Italian dress shoes and a handful of casuals, Gimme Shoes carries lines from Prada, Helmut Lang, Ted Baker and Michel Perry, to name a few. **Map p. 76, 3B** ❶

Paolo 524 Hayes St. (415) 552-4580, www.paoloshoes.com. Named for designer Paolo Iantorno, this shop takes Italian leather to the next level. Its classic shoes are handcrafted in Italy using specially selected leather and fabrics; kangaroo skin sandals and deerskin Mary Janes are quite nice. For a decorative touch, the shop's walls feature large masks from Venice. **Map p. 76, 3B** ❸

GIFTS & CRAFTS

The African Outlet 524 Octavia St., (415) 864-3576. This compact shop digs into the deepest parts of Africa for its colourful collection of masks, woven fabrics, ceremonial clothes, beads, musical instruments and antiques. Despite the store's small size, there is so much packed into the floor space that it's easy to get absorbed for hours, especially since the friendly owners enjoy describing each item in detail. The shop also rents some of its African outfits as costumes. **Map p. 76, 3B** ⑤

Flight 001 525 Hayes St., (415) 487-1084, www.flight001.com. Attempting to bring the glamour back into travel, Brad John and John Sencion opened their first Flight 001 in Greenwich Village. The Hayes Valley shop is shaped liked the hull of a 747 jetliner, with the register resembling a ticket counter and suitcases displayed in a baggage claim. Naturally, Flight 001 sells everything related to travel, including bags, guidebooks, globes and maps, as well as smaller necessary accessories, such as watches, stationery and aromatherapy products. Chic, designer bags like Tumi and Mandarina Duck are available. **Map p. 76, 3B** ③

Stitch 182 Gough St., (415) 431-3739, www.stitchlounge.com. Run by three women who were childhood friends, Stitch offers space for creative types looking to make their own clothes. Stitch describes itself as an urban sewing lounge, and is open to amateurs as well as seasoned sewing hands. Aside from use of their sewing machines, Stitch offers sewing classes and private lessons. There are also sewing experts available to answer questions. Some fabrics are available for purchase, as are old clothes that can be reworked into new designs. Stitch charges by the half hour. **Map p. 76, 3B** ①

True Sake 560 Hayes St., (415) 355-9555, www.truesake.com. With sake all the rage in San Francisco, it was only natural for sake connoisseur Beau Timken to create a shopping haven for fellow enthusiasts. True Sake is dedicated to this Japanese rice wine, catering to both the experienced as well as novice sake sipper. A large *sugidama*, a cedar ball made of cedar branches and traditionally hung by Japanese sake brewers, dangles outside the entrance. Inside, the sleek, Japanese modern shop features over 150 sakes from Japan, with prices ranging from about $10 to $200 a bottle. **Map p. 76, 3B** ③

Urban Knitting Studio 320 Fell St., (415) 552-5333, www.urban knitting.com. While the endless shelves of multi-hued yarn make for alluring eye candy, Urban Knitting Studio is much more than a yarn store. This space acts as a knitting collective where fellow knitters can share ideas in classes and workshops, all designed to spark creativity. The studio offers classes for beginners as well as dedicated hobbyists. There are a few pre-knitted scarves, sweaters and hats available, but the emphasis is on creating your own. **Map p. 76, 3B** ⑧

HOUSEWARES

Buu 506 Hayes St., (415) 626-1503. For those in the market for a sake set and Barbara Bui designer skirt, this eclectic shop fits the bill. The array of goods, mainly from Europe, Japan and America, includes glassware, candles, pocketknives, watches, women's clothes, silver jewellery, purses, body lotions and various fragrances. What ties Buu's seemingly random merchandise selection together is top-quality craftsmanship. **Map p. 76, 3B** ⑤

Champ de Mars 347 Hayes St., (415) 252-9434.This entire flea market of a shop pays homage to France, crammed with French-imported antiques and collectibles of every category, from decadent chandeliers to real French wine openers. Part of the fun is digging up gems, like an Eiffel Tower-shaped lamp or antique china. **Map p. 76, 3B** ②

Evelyn's Antique Chinese Furniture 381 Hayes St., (415) 255-1815. Evelyn's raises the bar when it comes to Chinese antique shops. It presents its exquisite pieces in a gallery-type setting and focuses on antique furniture from mainland China and from the 17th to the 19th C, with some 20th-C pieces. This is the spot to find a 19th-C black lacquer cabinet decorated with paintings from the Shanxi province for over $3,000 or a polychrome wood Buddha figure from the Qing Dynasty for $12,000. There are smaller items, like a set of 50-year-old red lacquer and leather pillows for $300. Evelyn's will arrange for custom pieces to be made to order in China. **Map p. 76, 3B** ②

F. Dorian 370 Hayes St., (415) 861-3191. Dorian features what it calls ethnic domestic antiques, mainly household items from South America, the Middle East, Africa and Asia. This includes items like a 18th-C Bolivian painting, a Teke magic figure from the Congo and a brass foot massager from India. Less expensive home items like Japanese rice bowls and contemporary cat pillows are available, as is a colourful selection of jewellery from around the world. **Map p. 76, 3B** ②

find 425 Hayes St., (415) 701-7100. Most of the sprawling retail space at this home and lifestyle store is devoted to furniture. The contemporary styles are warm and comfortable, with dark woods and silky quilts. There is also a selection of women's sportswear in a separate section of the store. **Map p. 76, 3B** ①

Friend 401 Hayes St., (415) 552-1717, www.friend-sf.com. Friend is much more than a home furnishings store; the eclectic items inside, many imported, are presented with enough flair to make shopping almost like a gallery visit. The shop was designed by Yves Behar, who also showcases his works inside. Other labels include Alessi, Kartell and Vitra, as well as locally made ceramics by Heath and lamps by Pablo. Friend also features changing art exhibits and hosts events that introduce designers to the public. **Map p. 76, 3B** ❶

Lavish 540 Hayes St., (415) 565-0540. Lavish proprietor Elizabeth Leu stocks unique yet functional items for the home. The boutique carries Lotta Jansdotter serving plates and creative vases, and colourful quilts and candles by Tocca. There is also a variety of handmade canvas tote bags, bath products and a whole line of baby gear, such as baby blankets, hats, diaper bags, books and crib bedding. **Map p. 76, 3B** ❸

Montauk 581 Hayes St., (415) 552-0930. Once you've taken a seat inside Montauk, it's hard to get up. The store, which specialises in custom-upholstered sofas and chairs, lures customers with its fluffy feather-and down-filled couches, loveseats and chairs. Prices range around the $3,500 mark for a couch. **Map p. 76, 3B** ❸

Propeller 555 Hayes St., (415) 701-7767. The ultramodern designs at Propeller incorporate a mix of materials, bold colours and motion-filled shapes. Catering to those with edgy tastes for in home design, this furniture shop mostly features new designers working in various media, including lighting, ceramics and woodwork. **Map p. 76, 3B** ❸

Worldware 336 Hayes St., (415) 487-9030, www.worldwaresf.com. This sophisticated interior design store boasts celebrity status, with customers including Sharon Stone, Dennis Miller, Danielle Steel and Richard Simmons. Designer and Worldware brainchild Greg Henson scans the globe for his collection of tasteful and eclectic home furnishings. Some items from the nearly 70 countries Henson works with include Havana-wood bookshelves, Buddha statues and pottery from Italy. **Map p. 76, 3B** ❷

Zonal 568 Hayes St., (415) 255-9307, www.zonalhome.com. Zonal's Hayes Valley location was its first. Owner Russell E. Pritchard's motto, 'Always repair, never restore', means the antiques in here remain charmingly weathered, occasionally with peeling paint and other minor flaws. Zonal sells vintage steel from the 1930s and 1940s and other collectible items. Much of the store's business, though, is with its inventory of modern furniture designs, such as new lamps, ottomans, sofas, dining room tables and chairs. **Map p. 76, 3B** ❸

THE HAIGHT

M.H. de Young Memorial Museum

OPEN	9.30 am–5.15 pm, Tue–Sun; until 8.45 pm, Fri. Last admission to special exhibits is one hour prior to closing.
CHARGES	$10 adults, $7 seniors, $6 ages 13–17 and college students with ID. Free admission the first Tuesday of the month. Special exhibits may have an extra charge. There is a $2 discount on admission with a MUNI transfer.
GUIDED VISITS	Audio tours of the permanent collection and special exhibitions are available, docent-led tours can be arranged in advance by calling (415) 682-2485.
DISABLED ACCESS	All entrances are accessible to the disabled, wheelchairs are available onsite.
SERVICES	Café located on ground level, museum store on ground level and lower level, coat check on lower level
TELEPHONE	(415) 863-3330
WEB	www.thinker.org
MAIN ENTRANCE	50 Tea Garden Drive, Golden Gate Park. Underground car park entrance at Fulton and 10th Ave.
GETTING THERE	#44 O'Shaughnessy bus to Music Concourse

HIGHLIGHTS
11th-C Dogon wood ancestor figure
Teotihuacan wall murals
8th-C lowland Maya Stela
Textiles, including the McCoy Jones collection
George and Dorothy Saxe Collection of Contemporary Craft
Rockefeller Collection of American Paintings
Marcia and John Friede New Guinea Collection

In 1894, San Francisco hosted the hectic, magnificent, tawdry and modern California Midwinter International Exposition in Golden Gate Park. *San Francisco Chronicle* publisher M.H. de Young, a strong promoter of the fair, was one of those interested in establishing a permanent museum as a memorial.

In March of 1895 the Memorial Museum opened with a collection of art and artefacts that had been assembled for the fair. For the next twenty years, de Young added to the collection though his own acquisitions, and in 1921 the museum name was changed to the M.H. de Young Memorial Museum, in tribute to de Young's years of patronage.

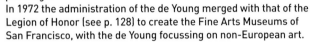

In 1972 the administration of the de Young merged with that of the Legion of Honor (see p. 128) to create the Fine Arts Museums of San Francisco, with the de Young focussing on non-European art.

THE BUILDING

The de Young was originally housed in an Egyptian-revival pavilion from the 1894 Midwinter Exhibition. In 1919, a larger Spanish Plateresque building was constructed. The Loma Prieta earthquake in 1989 caused structural damage to the building and in 2001 the old museum was demolished and construction begun on the new de Young. Designed by the Swiss firm of Herzog & de Meuron—Pritzker Prize winners known for their transformation of the Tate Modern in London—the new de Young is intended to harmonise with its natural setting. The building is covered in a skin of perforated copper panels meant to evoke light filtering through trees, and special courtyards filled with ferns and eucalyptus create an interplay between the museum and the surrounding park. Over time the copper exterior will age to a soft green, further blending into the environment.

A near doubling of gallery space in the new building allows for a much larger portion of the museum's holdings to be displayed, and rooms that have been designed around the collection. Several site-specific installations have been commissioned for the new museum, including work by Andy Goldsworthy, Gerhardt Richter and James Turrell. Towering over the building is one of the most notable features: the Harmon Education Tower spirals like a corkscrew, providing stunning views from ocean to bay.

The exterior of the new copper-clad de Young building

THE COLLECTIONS

The art of the de Young begins before you even enter the museum with a site-specific installation by **Andy Goldsworthy**. A crack in the stone that surrounds the museum begins at the roadway in front of the building and ascends the main walkway, cleaving boulders placed along its course, before ending at the entrance to the museum. Goldsworthy's commentary on the fault lines that run through California is particularly apt for a museum building that owes its existence to the destruction wrought by the Loma Prieta earthquake of 1989.

In the main court of the ground floor is another piece commissioned specifically for the new de Young building. **Gerhardt Richter**'s

DE YOUNG MUSEUM

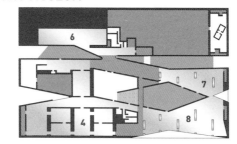

SECOND FLOOR

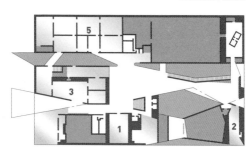

FIRST FLOOR

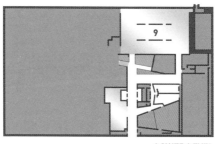

LOWER LEVEL

monumental mural is composed of 156 digitally manipulated photographs, a geometric motif in black and white that represents the atomic structure of strontium titanate, used to create artificial diamonds.

Adjacent to the main courtyard is the *FAMily room*, which houses ten California landscape murals by **Gottardo F. P. Piazzoni**. These murals were commissioned for the Main Library in the early 1930s, but with the transformation of that building into the Asian Art Museum (see p. 72) the murals were restored and transferred to the de Young.

Also in the main area of the ground floor is the *Children's Gallery*, which features computer-based interactive activities designed by the museum's education department as well as a viewing window that allows observation into the studio used by the museum's artists-in-residence. At weekends and in the afternoons visitors are encouraged to watch the artists at work.

Leaving the main court area, you have the option of ascending the staircase to reach the African, Oceanic, Early American Art and Textile galleries on the second floor, or continuing to explore the first-floor galleries, which cover Ancient Art of the Americas and 20th Century Art. Special exhibitions are located on the lower level. As the new de Young was designed to emphasise the connections between art of different eras and locales, there is no single recommended course through the galleries.

Directly behind the main court on the ground floor are the galleries containing the museum's collection of **ANCIENT AND NATIVE AMERICAN ART**, which has been a particular focus of the museum since its inception, some works dating back to the charter collection. The centrepiece of the collection is a series of bright, stylised *Teotihuacan murals* (500 of them). Located near present day Mexico City, Teotihuacan is the oldest city in North America (it was founded in 100 AD). A recently acquired highlight of this section is the *Lowland Maya Stela* (761). Carved from limestone, the piece is also known as the Vision Serpent stela and depicts a woman of royal rank, thought to be from Tikal or Dos Pilos.

From here you can enter the gallery devoted to **ART OF THE CRAFT**, or walk towards the main court for a more chronological

view of 20th-C art and the graphics collection. To view the
AMERICAN ART COLLECTION starting with colonial times, start on
the second floor, to the right of the main staircase.

Galleries 11 and 12 contain displays from the museum's
Achenbach Foundation for the Graphic Arts, the most
comprehensive collection of works of art on paper in the western
United States. Included in the graphics collection are the archives
of San Francisco's Crown Point Press (see p. 30), acquired by the
museum in 1991, which contains prints by **Richard Diebenkorn**,
Helen Frankenthaler, **Sol LeWitt** and **Wayne Thiebaud**.

The roots and development of modern American art and its
impact on contemporary art are explored in *Galleries 13 and 14*.
The contribution of **Alfred Stieglitz** and his contemporaries to the
burgeoning modern art movement is considered, as well as artists
such as **Diego Rivera** whose work does not adhere to the New York
style of modernism. Also in this gallery is an in-depth look at the
work of Japanese American artist **Chiura Obata**, whose California
landscapes blend an Asian influence with American subject matter.

Gallery 15 focuses on American Regionalism and Social Realism
during the 1930s and 1940s, with paintings such as **John Marin**'s
Study, New York (1934) and **John Langley Howard**'s *Embarcadero
and Clay Street* (1935) offering views of the urban landscape and
the Great Depression. Also included are paintings by African
American artists such as **Claude Clark** and **Aaron Douglas**.

The following room explores Abstract Expressionism, noting the
cultural differences between the New York and San Francisco
branches of the movement. The works of California artists such as
Richard Diebenkorn, **Frank Lobdell** and **Jay De Feo** are included
here, as well as paintings by artists from the New York school.

Gallery 16 reflects the politically charged environment of the 1960s
with art that speaks to the politics of the time. **Jack Levine**'s
Birmingham '63 addresses the civil rights movement, while **Cleve
Gray**'s *Reverend Quan Duc* (1963) tackles the Vietnam War protests.

The increasingly global context of the world of art is explored in
the following gallery with works such as **Masami Teraoka**'s
American Kabuki/Oishiiwa (1986), a blend of Japanese ukiyo-e print
and Pop aesthetics. In **Robert Colescott**'s *Brown Grandmother of the*

George Caleb Bingham *Boatmen on the Missouri* (1846)

Year (1994) racial stereotypes of African Americans are explored through images taken from mainstream media.

Closing the series of American Art is a gallery devoted to the Art of the Craft. **Clifford Rainey**'s *Fetish* (1990) is an oversized Coke bottle transformed into an African power figure, while **Kiki Smith**'s wall hanging—commissioned specifically for the new museum building—is inspired by Lucy, the three-million-year-old skeleton that provided scientists with the missing link in human evolution.

A chronological survey of the museum's holdings of **AMERICAN ART** begins on the second floor, to the right of the staircase. The first gallery explores the cultural interplay between Native Americans and the colonial settlers who emigrated from Europe with paintings like *Fire in a Missouri Meadow and a Party of Sioux Indians Escaping From It, Upper Missouri* by George Catlin (1871). **George Caleb Bingham**'s *Boatmen on the Missouri* (1846) is a gem of the collection (see picture above).

Gallery 2 looks at the influence of both the Colonial and the Colonial Revival Movement. **Charles Sheeler**'s painting of antiques in Kitchen, Williamsburg (1937) was a special commission by the Rockefeller family, which was interested in promoting appreciation for the Colonial period.

Gallery 5 explores the negotiation of the American identity following the declaration of independence from Great Britain. Various works, such as a copy of the famous **Gilbert Stuart** portrait of George Washington used on the dollar bill (c. 1854), look at the evolution of Washington as an icon.

Gallery 4 focuses on the expansion of the United States in the years preceding the American Civil War. Paintings such as *Peter Quivey and the Mountain Lion* (1856), by **Charles Christian Nahl**, attest to the expansion westward, while **Albert Bierstadt**'s *Roman Fish Market, Arch of Octavius* (1858), shows American travellers seeking the sophistication of the old world. An interesting installation is a comparison of austere Shaker furniture with furniture in the Rococo Revival style.

The following gallery focuses on the concepts of real and ideal. Realism is represented by **Thomas Waterman Wood**'s *Cogitation* (1871) and **Thomas Anshutz**'s *Ironworkers' Noontime* (1880). Romanticism takes over in **Elihu Vedder**'s seductive *Sphinx of the Seashore* (1879).

Gallery 6 explores America's interest in the still life and trompe l'oeil. Symbolism and science in still life is investigated through works such as **Raphaelle Peale**'s *Blackberries* (c. 1813), while the genre is brought into the modern by *Still Life with Grape Juice and Sandwiches* (1997), by **David Ligare**. The whimsy of trompe l'oeil is shown through pieces such as *After the Hunt* (1885) by **William Michael Harnett** and *Salmon Trout and Smelt* (1873) by **Samuel Marsden Brookes**. Also included amongst the trompe l'oeil is *Samuel Marsden Brookes in His Studio* (1876) by **Edwin Deakin**.

The following gallery is devoted to the art of the Hudson River School, and explores how the American landscape became a metaphor for the aspirations and identity of a new country. Paintings by **Thomas Cole** as well as **Frederic E. Church**'s *Rainy Season in the Tropics* (1866) depict a sublime beauty to be found in nature, while **Albert Bierstadt**'s *California Spring* (1875) shows the state as a pastoral Eden, touched by a heavenly light. An ironic counterpoint to this is **Sandow Birk**'s faux Hudson River School painting of *Fog Over San Quentin State Prison, San Quentin, California* (2001), which suggests that the apple of the golden state may have a rotten core.

The transitional area that follows *Gallery 7* looks at the roots and development of the American Barbizon movement, including work by **Jean-Baptiste-Camille Corot**.

Gallery 9 explores the work of American Impressionists as well as the Ashcan school. Look for portraits by **John Singer Sargent** and **John Singleton Copley** as well as **Mary Cassat**'s portrait of *Mrs. Robert Cassat, the Artist's Mother* (1889). The next gallery is devoted to the American Arts and Crafts Movement, which was influenced both by a reaction to the industrial revolution and by an increased awareness of international cultures.

(Those who wish to continue with a chronological survey of American Art can now go to the 20th-C galleries on the first floor.)

Also on the second floor is the museum's textile collection. Though the textile displays are rotated on a regular basis, some of the collection's highlights to look for include European tapestries, Uzbek embroideries, the most important group of Anatolian kilims outside of Turkey and an excellent costume collection (18th C to present day).

The textiles area leads to a Connections Gallery, an area devoted to work by contemporary artists responding to pieces in the museum collection. These site-specific installations speak to tradition from a modern day viewpoint and create a link between past and present.

Continuing on leads you to the Oceanic Art area. Both the African and Oceanic Art galleries were designed by Herzog & de Meuron to be open, free-flowing spaces.

The African Art collection covers over 20 countries, and the 11th to the 21st C. The African Art selections are displayed thematically, allowing the visitor to appreciate regional differences while also understanding the commonalities.

The strengths of the African collection are the holdings from the Dogon and Yoruba. In particular, look for the sculpture of a standing

Claes Oldenberg and Coosje van Bruggen *Corridor Pin, Blue* (1999)

Dogon figure (1200), one of the earliest known wood ancestor figures from Mali. Another significant piece is the *Mask of a Hornbill Bird* decorated with Arabic inscriptions, from the Mano people of Liberia (19th C). From the Kongo people of Central Africa comes an early *Nail and Blade Oath-Taking Figure* (19th C). Each village had one such figure, which was kept in a special shrine outside the village; each nail or blade inserted into the figure stands for a quarrel that was settled.

Oceanic Art was one of the first collections of the museum, and has expanded; the Marcia and John Friede Collection, in particular, contains a comprehensive collection of the art of Papua New Guinea. The Oceanic collection also includes the Hemingway collection of Australian Aboriginal Art and the Gantner Myer Collection of contemporary Aboriginal Art.

Adjacent to the museum, and accessible through the ground floor exit next to the café, is the museum's Barbro Osher Sculpture Garden, designed by noted landscape architect Walter Hood. Sculpture highlights include *Corridor Pin, Blue* (1999) by **Claes Oldenberg** and **Coosje van Bruggen** (see picture opposite); *Ocean Gate* (1982) by **Louise Nevelson**; *Pierced Monolith with Color* (1965) by **Barbara Hepworth**; and an untitled piece by **Isamu Noguchi** (1978).

The final site-specific commission for the new de Young is **James Turrell**'s *Three Gems* (2004), an underground chamber with a light-influenced view of the sky.

in the area

GOLDEN GATE PARK

This three-mile strip of land, once dominated by desolate sand dunes, was reclaimed in the 1870s to create San Francisco's largest park. Boasting lakes, gardens, memorials, sports fields, two Dutch windmills and even a herd of bison, this recreational oasis is nearly as diverse as the city that surrounds it.

Conservatory of Flowers John F. Kennedy Drive. Open 9 am–4.30 pm, Tue–Sun. $5/$3, free on first Tuesday of the month. This greenhouse nurtures a thicket of plant life, including water lilies six feet in diameter and insect-eating 'pitcher plants'. From downtown, take the #5, 7, 21 or 71 bus, or take the N-Judah streetcar. **Map p. 100, 2A**

Japanese Tea Garden Open 8.30 am–6 pm, Mon–Sun. Admission $3.50/$1.25. The oldest Japanese garden in the US. Winding paths among bonsai trees and ponds of carp highlight the charm of Japanese landscaping, while a tiny teahouse serves refreshments. Even amidst its steady stream of visitors, the Tea Garden retains the power to calm the harried urban soul. **Map p. 100, 1B**

commercial galleries

Café Evolution 1336 9th Ave (between Irving and Judah), (415) 665-4840, www.cafeevolution.com. Part-owned by a local artist, Café Evolution focuses on accessible and affordable art in a relaxed environment. The art tends towards smaller pieces in acrylic and oils, the staff is friendly, and even beginning collectors will be put at ease. **Map p. 100, 1C** ❶

Canvas Gallery and Café 1200 9th Ave. (at Lincoln), (415) 504-0060, www.thecanvasgallery.com. Part café bar, part art gallery, Canvas shows local artists. Many exhibits are themed and evening entertainment—from DJs to live music to poetry slams—keeps the atmosphere lively and the room full. A twice-monthly Feria Urbana offers a variety of crafts made by local designers in a multi-artist trunk show. **Map p. 100, 1C** ❷

Gallery 683 683 Haight St., (415) 861-1311. Gallery 683 has a split personality. On one hand, the shop features tribal art from Central and South America, as well as from Southern Mexico. Native American crafts, such as jewellery and drums, are available as well. At the same time, Gallery 683 hawks a seemingly unrelated collection of original 1960s rock posters, handbills, and memorabilia. **Off map**

Upper Playground and Fifty24SF Gallery 220 Fillmore St. (between Haight and Waller), (415) 571-0187, www.upperplayground.com. This is one gallery with street cred. The space consists of an art gallery called Fifty24SF, a

The Japanese Tea Garden

ase SAN FRANCISCO

clothing store and a back room full of used vinyl, mainly soul and jazz. Regular exhibitions by local and national artists including Sam Flores and Albert Reyes. Take the #71 bus. **Off map**

eat

$ **Axum Cafe** 698 Haight St., (415) 252-7912. 5 pm–10.30 pm, Mon–Fri; from 1 pm, Sat–Sun. The denizens of Lower Haight love this humble little Ethiopian joint. There's nothing much to say about the decor, because it really doesn't have any. But it does offer tasty and authentic Ethiopian fare in large portions at low prices. Down to your last dollar? Eat here. But come early to avoid a wait. **Map p. 100, 3B** ❶

Cha Cha Cha 1801 Haight St., (415) 386-5758. Open 11.30 am–4 pm every day; again from 5 pm–11 pm, Sun–Thur; and until 11.30, Fri–Sat. Don't come here to be calm and relaxed. Come here to have loud, lively fun. Even the house's answering machine message is shouted. But it's hugely popular, doesn't take reservations, and there is usually a long wait in the crowded (and did we mention loud?) bar. Caribbean specialities such as red snapper steamed in banana leaf are mainstays. The wine list is short, but the house sangria is good. **Map p. 100, 3-4B** ❷

Kate's Kitchen 471 Haight St., (415) 626-3984. Open 8 am–9 pm, Mon–Fri; 9 am–9 pm, Sat; 9 am–9 pm, Sun. Like many—perhaps most—places to eat in the Haight, Kate's is an unassuming café catering to neighbourhood folk who are looking for an inexpensive, ample meal and not a restaurant experience. Kate's has a southern cooking (Dixie) influence and specialises in breakfast food. The huge pancakes are a local favourite. **Map p. 100, 4B** ❸

Massawa Restaurant 1538 Haight St., (415) 621-4129. Open 11.30 am–10 pm, Sun–Thur; until 11 pm, Fri–Sat. This Ethiopian restaurant will take no prize for decor, but the wide storefront windows make for good people-watching in one of the city's more colourful neighbourhoods. They'll give you a fork if you really want one, but the custom here—as in Ethiopia—is eat with your hand. Break off a piece of the flat, spongy injera bread and use it to scoop up the delicious vegetables, chopped meats and legume purees. **Map p. 76, 2C** ❹

Pork Store Café 1451 Haight St., (415) 864-6981. Open 7 am–3.30 pm, Mon–Fri; 8.30 am–4 pm, Sat–Sun. This little hole-in-the-wall, truck-stop style café—in operation since 1919—does not rely for its success on looking pretty. Nor do they waste money on the grooming and training of the waiters. But take a seat at one of the rickety tables and enjoy one of the best deals (penny for penny) in town. You'll get all the elements of a traditional American breakfast: eggs, bacon, hash browns, pancakes and coffee. For lunch it's burgers, fries and other tasty piles of cholesterol. **Map p. 76, 2C** ❺

Rockin' Java 1821 Haight St., (415) 831-8842. Open 10 am–10 pm. A coffee house-cum-social club, with pool table, pinball, internet and the music of local musicians, such as swing diva Lavay Smith. The comfortable design, with round tables, cosy couches and stuffed chairs, make it a perfect refuge from fatigue. **Map p. 76, 2C** ❻

Squat & Gobble Café 237 Fillmore St., (415) 487-0551. Open 8 am–10 pm. Despite the idiotic name, legions of locals fill the large, airy interior. They turn up because of the ample portions and low prices: not only do they come here for the tasty crêpes (the house speciality), omelettes, salads and sandwiches, but also just to while away an afternoon with coffee and the newspaper. The menu is posted on the wall and includes many good vegetarian items. **Map p. 100, 3B** ❼

Thep Phanom 400 Waller St., (415) 431-2526. Open 5.30 pm–10.30 pm. Widely regarded as one of the best Thai restaurants in its price range, Thep Phanom is patronised by a continually changing cast of characters from all walks of city life. Pepper-marinated crispy-fried quail is a speciality, as is spicy mushroom salad. But most of the menu is predictable, with all the Thai regulars such as Pad Thai with prawns. It's a tightly packed little space, but ornately decorated with wall paintings and gilt. **Off map** ❽

Zam Zam 1633 Haight St., (415) 861-2545. Open 2 pm–2 am. With he most incongruous enterprise and the oddest decor in all the Haight-Ashbury district, the Zam Zam is a cocktail lounge right out of the 1950s: plush and lush and decadent with a Persian theme. Even during the crazy years, the Zam Zam was a thriving throwback that continued to shake Martinis and stir Manhattans all through the psychedelic 1960s. The Flower Children are gone, but Zam Zam is still here. **Map p. 76, 2C** 🟢

shop

This parkside neighbourhood of run-down Victorian houses witnessed the birth of the hippie movement. Communal living, free love and psychedelia attracted tens of thousands of young people from across the country, culminating in 1967's 'Summer of Love.' Rock legends made Haight-Ashbury their home, including ur-jam band the Grateful Dead (at 710 Ashbury St.) and blues wailer Janis Joplin.The spirit of the1960s no longer lingers in the air here (the occasional scent of cannabis notwithstanding), but college-age bohemians still predominate, and the many vintage-clothing stores, cafés and record shops lend the area an alternative feel. Start at Golden Gate Park and walk down Haight St. to the corner of Ashbury (the intersection of fame). If you keep going, you'll walk down a hill into Lower Haight, which has a distinctly grittier feel.

BOOKS

Booksmith 1644 Haight St., (415) 863-8688. Opened in 1976, the Booksmith has become something of a Haight institution. The likes of Gary Larson and Allen Ginsberg have appeared at this independent bookstore. Along with a vast selection of new books and magazines, Booksmith sells spoken-word CDs and offers author readings and events up to twice a week. Since it is a destination store for touring authors, Booksmith offers many signed first editions of recently published works. **Map p. 100, 3B** 🔴

Bound Together Anarchist Collective 1369 Haight St., (415) 431-8355. Bound Together, which first opened in 1976, is a volunteer-run business.

Rather than stock mainstream paperbacks, books here address issues of globalisation, vegetarianism, gay rights and left-wing interpretations of foreign affairs. There are also piles of independently released journals and fanzines chronicling everything from the punk rock scene in Europe to the degradation of the environment. The collective also organises the annual Bay Area Anarchist Bookfair. **Map p. 100, 4B** ❷

CLOTHES
THRIFT & VINTAGE

Haight is a mecca for vintage and thrift shoppers. They come here not to get clothes on the cheap, but rather in hopes of finding that perfect, unworn Dior dress or just the right shape of orange polyester pants.

Aaardvark's Odd Ark 1501 Haight St., (415) 621-3141. It's difficult to pass by the colourful display of vintage wear without stopping into Aaardvark's. Racks and racks are filled with inexpensive used clothing, focusing on retro, often quirky styles. Though much of the stock is casual, you can find some things to go with the feather boas. **Map p. 100, 4B** ❸

Crossroads Trading Co. 1519 Haight St., (415) 355-0555, www.crossroads trading.com. To call Crossroads a used-clothing store does not do it justice. This Bay Area chain offers an expansive showroom of designer and high-quality used goods, many of which can pass as new. The Haight Street location caters to its youthful customer base by offering trendy, club-ready options. **Map p. 100, 4B** ❸

Held Over 1543 Haight St., (415) 864-0818. The used clothes at Held Over are organised by decade. Both men and women can dig through the stock here for everything from zoot suits to 1980s-style camouflage fatigues. The vintage-wear at Held Over is moderately priced, especially considering the high quality. **Map p. 100, 4B** ❸

La Rosa Vintage 1711 Haight St., (415) 668-3744. La Rosa Vintage adds a touch of class to the Haight. The vintage wear tends toward the upscale, focusing on clothes and collectables from the 1920s–1950s. All items, whether they are flapper dresses, formal gowns, dinner jackets or leisure suits, are in perfect condition. La Rosa also displays a vast selection of vintage jewellery and other accessories. **Map p. 100, 3B** ❹

Static 1764 Haight St., (415) 422-0046. Those nostalgic for their 1970s and 1980s wardrobes can relive fringe shirts and skinny ties at Static. This vintage boutique carries 1970s-style denim, Adidas jackets as well as Pucci dresses. Static also sells fur jackets as well as vintage accessories such as old Gucci purses and 1980s Cure concert buttons. **Map p. 100, 3B** ❹

Wasteland 1660 Haight St., (415) 863-3150. A staple for Haight St. shoppers, Wasteland is the quintessential vintage clothing store, spanning all eras. Used clothes can range from a 1940s formal gown to 1970s polyester. Used goods here are often fun and funky, including vinyl skirts. For the less adventurous, Wasteland offers plenty of basic sweaters, dresses, jackets and used Levis. Accessories include big and chunky jewellery as well as new sunglasses and wigs. **Map p. 100, 3B** ⑤

NEW CLOTHES

Ambiance 1458 Haight St., (415) 552-5095. Ambiance oozes girly urban chic. Fashion hounds tapping into their feminine side can find the latest styles from the likes of Trina Turk, Luscious, Weston Wear, Hype and Sweet Pea. Ambiance can also provide an entire wardrobe for a black tie event, wedding or prom, accessories included. **Map p. 100, 4B** ⑥

Behind the Post Office 1510 Haight St., (415) 861-2507. Co-owners Stephen Pringle and Kim Baskind choose their labels wisely for this men's and women's boutique. The duo opt for smaller, independent designers that focus on smart styles and form fit; labels like Buka and Development provide a trend-setting aesthetic. Behind the Post Office (it's not behind one) also offers casual T-shirts and jeans. **Map p. 100, 4B** ③

Cheap Thrills 1324 Haight St., (415) 252-8395; 1687 Haight St., (415) 252-5687. New York transplants, missing the punk scene of the 1970s and 1980s, will find a haven at both Cheap Thrills stores. Cheap Thrills hawks all the old-school paraphernalia, including punk T-shirts, CBGB tank tops and bright green hair dye. Aside from the retro punk fare, Cheap Thrills sells silly gift items, such as Pez dispensers, Garbage Pail Kids stickers and Bendy toys. **Map p. 100, 4B** ②

Clobba 1604 Haight St., (415) 864-4701. A sanctuary for the young and hip, Clobba caters for teen and twenty-somethings with fun urban designs, mainly from New York and Los Angeles, Clobba can dress you for a casual evening or a night of clubbing, and the key is affordability. Clobba has several other locations in the city. **Map p. 100, 3B** ⑤

Costumes on Haight 735 Haight St., (415) 621-1356. Halloween lasts year-round at this costume outlet. Rather than pre-packaged outfits, much of the stock here is sold as separates, designed to stimulate people's creative edge. The shop is crammed with every accoutrement imaginable, including Renaissance wear, pimp jackets, feather boas, poodle skirts, a full selection of masks, superhero outfits and more. If the costume is for a one-off event, there is an option to rent. **Off map**

Daljeets 1773 Haight St., (415) 668-8500, www.daljeets.com. For more than 30 years, Daljeets has been dressing its Haight Street clientele in glam, rockabilly, punk and gothic clothes, with an emphasis on fetish wear. For the ladies, there are corsets, sexy club wear and provocative Hustler undies. Guys can find club and punk shirts. Its shoe selection varies from motorcycle boots to trendy club gear, and Daljeets also specialises in funky platform shoes for men and women. **Map p. 100, 3B ➍**

Jaxx 1584 Haight St., (415) 869-1070. Since its inception in early 2002, Jaxx has caused quite a buzz on the fashion scene in San Francisco. Some of the designers that work with this high fashion boutique create styles that are exclusive to Jaxx and the inviting store layout and clientele round out the pleasant experience. **Map p. 100, 3B ➎**

Kweejibo Clothing Co. 1580 Haight St., (415) 552-3555, www.kweejibo.com. Taking its name from an early episode of the Simpsons, Kweejibo adds a sleek, casual look to any wardrobe. Shop owner Cindy Cho designs the Kweejibo line of men's shirts, using some synthetics, but also silk and linen, and the whole lot is made locally. Cho often opts for deep colours to highlight her designs. **Map p. 100, 3B ➎**

New York Apparel 1772 Haight St., (415) 751-8823. As an antidote to some of Haight's lingering hippie-era shops, New York Apparel brings in a breath of East Coast cool. The store likes to flash its vinyl black mini-dress, fishnet bodysuit, lace corset, bondage pants, mini-kilt and 1980s-era opaque striped and coloured tights. New York punk wear, like studded belts and bracelets, also lives on here. The shop always has a good sales rack in the back. **Map p. 100, 3B ➍**

Piedmont Boutique 1452 Haight St., (415) 864-8075, www.piedmontsf.com. Every day is dress-up day at Piedmont, which has been a Haight Street institution for more than 30 years. Patrons are welcomed by two giant legs sticking out over the store's entrance, a small hint at the eccentricities found inside. Uti, Piedmont's designer, creates most of the formal evening gowns, hot pants, feather jackets, strapless bustiers and capes. For those who want to accessorise, Piedmont offers plenty of rhinestone jewellery, feather boas, cigarette holders and satin gloves. Piedmont's seamstresses can produce anything on request in just a couple of days, and often outfits local performers. **Map p. 100, 4B ➏**

True 1415 Haight St., (415) 626-2882; 1427 Haight St., (415) 626-2331; 1429 Haight St., (415) 626-2600. True is beginning to have a monopoly on Haight St. There are three True shops—one for men, one for women, one for shoes (called True Sole). All three provide garb that could be worn by club DJs and other casual urban fashion hounds. Some of the labels represented include Enyce, Ecko, Akademiks, Mecca and Babyphat. True's own line of clothes is mostly confined to T-shirts, sweatshirts, and jeans. **Map p. 100, 4B** ④

Villains 1672 Haight St., (415) 626-5939; **Villains Vault** at 1653 Haight St., (415) 864-7727. Standing out as one of the Haight's best shops, Villains caters to slightly different markets with its two locations. The main store caters to skaters, surfers and hip-hop kids with a mix of brand-name and alternative labels, including Greed Girl, Paul Frank, Fresh Jive, Doll House, Hurley, Volcom and French Connection. Across the street, Villains Vault offers higher-end, more conservative attire, filling the shelves with Diesel, Kenneth Cole, Theory and Miss Sixty. **Map p. 100, 3B** ①

SHOES

John Fluevog Shoes 1697 Haight St., (415) 436-9784, www.fluevog.com. Designer John Fluevog produces a line of innovative yet wearable and sturdy shoes in an array of designs (including the Angel line, which are 'Satan-resistant'). Women can find magenta and black funky uppers, lemon-yellow, slip-on rubber-soled wedgies, and red lace-up boots. Mens' shoe options include the black and blue wing-tip and black box-toe leather uppers. There are a number of unisex options as well. If you're here in January or the summer, you could catch a big sale. **Map p. 100, 3B** ①

Luichiny 1529 Haight St., (415) 252-7065, www.luichiny.com. For anyone looking to get their feet noticed, Luichiny provides ample opportunity. The motto seems to be the more outlandish the better, with platforms that look the size of a Manhattan skyscraper. Luichiny's eccentric boots, like its leopard-print lace-ups and its glittery stilettos, can be worn by club-goers, drag queens, strippers and even ladies of the night. Luichiny does carry more tame dress shoes. Prices for the wacky designs can also be outlandish. **Map p. 100, 4B** ③

Shoe Biz Inc. 1422 Haight St., (415) 861-0313; 1446 Haight St., (415) 864-0990; 1553 Haight St., (415) 861-3933. Shoe Biz opened its doors on Haight St. in 1979 and now has three locations. Each offers trendy footwear at affordable prices, but each is a bit different. Shoe Biz at 1446 Haight reaches out to the club kids with brands like Steve Madden and Dr. Martens. Shoe Biz II at 1553 Haight features Adidas and Puma sneakers as well as skate shoes. The largest location, Super Shoe Biz at 1422 Haight, focuses on a more dressy style with European imports and higher-end labels. **Map p. 100, 4B** ⑥

MUSIC

Amoeba Music 1855 Haight St., (415) 831-1200, www.amoeba records.com. The motherlode of all San Francisco record stores, Amoeba Music is a full-day destination for music lovers. This is the place to find that rare tribal CD from Ethiopia as well as the latest entries in the alternative rock world. And Yugoslavian brass bands? Of course. Customers can buy, sell and trade at Amoeba, a local Berkeley store made good and still expanding. Used CDs are in excellent condition, and new offerings are often at sale prices. **Map p. 100, 3B** 7

Ceiba 1364 Haight St., (415) 437-9598, www.ceibarec.com. Ceiba melds music and art at its Haight St. outlet. The store's main focus is its record label, featuring downtempo, trance, ambient and break beats. Aside from the music, Ceiba displays visual arts from independent artists and producers, and offers ravers some colourful, alternative clothes and accessories. **Map p. 100, 4B** 2

Future Primitive Sound 597 Haight St., (415) 551-2328, www.future primitivesound.com. Aside from acting as a music outlet, this locale is the headquarters of the Future Primitive Sound art collective. The shop is a record store, gallery and clothing shop all in one, featuring the music, art, and fashion designs developed by the collective's artists. Hip-hop culture plays a large part in the music releases as well as art presented here. Future Sound offers works from Japanese-born painter Kenji, urban streetwear designed by renowned graffiti artists Doze Green, and even books on hip-hop culture. **Off map**

Groove Merchant 687 Haight St., (415) 252-5766. Just browsing at Groove Merchant is entertainment in itself. This is the place to learn about the roots of today's music, with racks of old-school funk, soul and jazz music. Some of the items are rare collectibles. **Off map**

Recycled Records 1377 Haight St., (415) 626-4075. Unsurprisingly, used CDs and records are Recycled's niche. Collectors also come here for the rare 45s and albums, but as technology changes the industry, Recycled has increased its stock to sell a variety of collectibles, such as vintage theatre programs, turn-of-the-century sheet music, old rock posters and even original Barbie dolls. **Map p. 100, 4B** 2

Rooky Ricardo's 448 Haight St., (415) 864-7526, www.rookyricardos records.com. Vinyl is not just a faded memory at Rooky Ricardo's. The liquorice pizza lives on in the form of soul, Motown, funk, jazz, reggae and blues. Rooky's is also known for its selection of over 50,000 old 45s, include R&B and funk singles. The shop is adorned with whimsical murals. Collectors will not get gouged here on prices. **Off map**

Tweekin' Records 593 Haight St., (415) 626-6995, www.tweekin.com. Though Tweekin' does a lot of online business, there is nothing quite like previewing and testing the CDs and vinyl in person. Tweekin' specialises in dance music, including progressive trance, break beat, drum & bass or tribal house. The store also sells a line of Tweekin' T-shirts, bags and other accessories. **Off map**

GIFTS, ACCESSORIES & OTHER

Body Time 1465 Haight St., (415) 551-1070, www.bodytime.com. Originally opening as the Body Shop in 1970 (before selling its name to the English company), Body Time takes a personal approach to beautifying its customers. Bath and body products, all made in Berkeley, include massage oils, chai soap bars, lavender exfoliating pouches, children's body paint and aromatherapy lamps. Custom-made scents are a speciality, and perfume oils can be blended and added to lotions and other body products. Customers can take samples of products home to make sure they work. **Map p. 100, 4B** ⑥

Dreams of Kathmandu 1352 Haight St., (415) 255-4968. The purple-and-green façade makes Dreams of Kathmandu hard to miss. Inside, the inventory is a bit more sedate, with Tibetan prayer flags hanging from the ceiling, Buddha and elephant statues on the shelves and Nepalese paper lanterns, batiks, jewellery, masks and incense boxes adding to the atmosphere. Quality cashmere wraps are sold, as are CDs of Tibetan and Nepalese music. **Map p. 100, 4B** ❷

Egg 85 Carl St., (415) 564-2248. The hodgepodge of goods found at egg loosely fall under the category of housewares. The store's eclectic stock makes perfect gift items for those hard-to-shop-for friends; you can find anything from a wine rack made from industrial tubes to a designer oil and vinegar set. Though some of the items are made by local artists, egg also carries a variety of international goods: for instance, a multi-egg holder from France and a British toast rack. Scattered about are books on faeries and kings, forest gnomes, and other odd subject matter. **Map p. 100, 3C** ❽

Giant Robot 622 Shrader St., (415) 876-GRSF, www.gr-sf.com. The store carries Japanese graphic design books, American indie comics, Japanese-American artist-designed T-shirts, and local Bay Area e-zines. Giant Robot also carries a large selection of Japanese Kubricks miniature figure toys. **Map p. 100, 3B** ❾

Kidrobot 1512 Haight St., (415) 487-9000, www.kidrobot.com. One of the hot spots on San Francisco's extensive Asian pop culture scene, Kidrobot specialises in Urban Vinyl figures, one of today's most popular toy genres. Renowned artists such as Michael Lau, Eric So and ITRangers have created much of the Kidrobot collectible fare. Toys also include Kubricks plastic miniatures, Gloomy Bears from toy designer Cube-Works, Murakami DOB dolls and US-made plush figures. Much of the Kidrobot stock is custom-made in limited quantities. **Map p. 100, 4B** ③

Land of the Sun 1715 Haight St., (415) 831-8646. Flower Power lives on here. Land of the Sun carries the typical 1960s Summer of Love gear, including tie-dye shirts, Jerry Garcia wall hangings, peace necklaces, Haight-Ashbury T-shirts, Janis Joplin photos, candles and incense. It is also a good spot for gift items, such as wooden jewellery boxes, glass and wood pipes, lava lamps and old playbills. **Map p. 100, 3B** ④

Mendel's Art Supplies 1556 Haight St., (415) 621-1287, www.mendels.com. While all around has shifted and changed, Mendel's has managed to ride the economic turbulence of the Haight, remaining one of the street's oldest tenants. What started out in 1968 as mainly a house paint store has over the years diversified along with the community and become a full art supply outlet. Mendel's also carries offbeat costumes and eccentric fabrics, as well as craft items like origami kits, stickers, paint, paper, and rubber stamps. **Map p. 100, 3B** ⑤

Mickey's Monkey 214 Pierce St., (415) 864-0693. There's no telling what knick-knacks will be found at Mickey's Monkey. The small shop, hidden off the main street, is crammed with all sorts of collectibles: lava lamps, globes, wooden crosses, masks, turtle lights and other trinkets, all neatly displayed in the space available. It's also a place to find used furniture at decent prices. **Off map**

PlanetWeavers 1573 Haight St., (415) 864-4415, www.planet weavers.com. A stroll through this spacious store is a walk through politically correct territory. The long aisles flow with ecologically and spiritually minded items. This is the place to stock up on African drums, Buddha statues, didgeridoos, Indonesian masks and bonsai kits. All this between rows of religious books, Tarot cards, aromatherapy handbooks and fairy dust. **Map p. 100, 3B** ⑤

Positively Haight Street 1400 Haight St., (415) 252-8747. The blast of incense you inhale upon entering the store reveals as much about the store's merchandise as does the shop's name. Positively Haight Street lingers in the bygone hippie era with its hemp bracelets, Grateful Dead photos and T-shirts, mushroom candles and hand-blown glass pipes. It also offers knit hats, dresses and skirts from India and other imports from Thailand, India and Nepal. **Map p. 100, 4B** ⑩

Off the Wall 1669 Haight St., (415) 863-8170. What's on the wall is what's important at this poster shop. One side of Off the Wall focuses on artist-drawn concert posters, mainly limited editions and signed, numbered and silk-screened specimens. The other half of the store spotlights vintage French posters, black-and-white photos of old movie stars and fine art prints. All posters are in mint condition and can be purchased with a frame or custom-framed at the gallery. **Map p. 100, 3B** ❶

Revival of the Fittest 1701 Haight St., (415) 751-8857. A variety shop in every sense of the word, Revival of the Fittest emphasises diversity. Hand-painted martini glasses, turtle lamps, Curious George magnets, butterfly candles, Playboy swizzle sticks, jewellery, hats, coats, Peruvian sweaters, purses and other accessories are just a few of the items available here. **Map p. 100, 3B** ❹

Stuf 1612 Haight St., (415) 551-STUF. Stuf lives and dies by the law that one must accessorise. This is one-stop shopping to help liven up any outfit with a handbag, shoes, hat or colourful jewellery. Everything here is frivolous and fun. **Map p. 100, 3B** ❺

The Sword and Rose 85 Carl St., (415) 681-5434. For those into the occult or with a penchant for the underworld, the more-than-20-year-old Sword and Rose is your store. Inside are crystals, Tarot cards, Buddhas, incense and many a talisman. You can also have a reading done by one of the staff. Closed Mondays. **Map p. 100, 3C** ❽

Tibet Styles 1707 Haight St., (415) 387-0903. Though Tibet Styles is not all that different from San Francisco's ubiquitous Tibetan and Nepalese shops, the layout is inviting and the quality of goods higher than most. The shop is filled with rugs, jewellery, jackets and wall hangings. The stock in this outlet is designed mostly by Tibetan refugees who live in India and Nepal. A few nice touches in the store make a difference, such as offering insight and information about the symbols on each of the wall hangings. **Map p. 100, 3B** ❹

CLEMENT ST.
& THE RICHMOND
DISTRICT

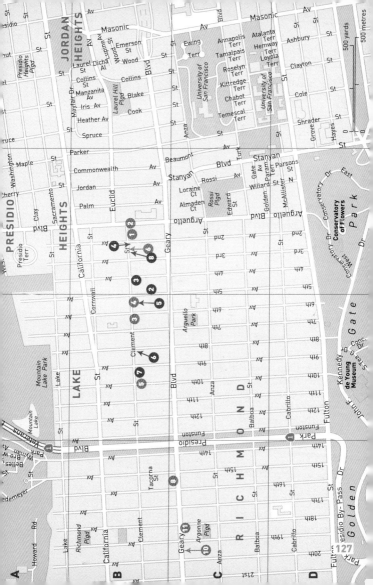

California Palace of the Legion of Honor

OPEN	9.30 am–5 pm, Tue–Sun
CHARGES	$8 adults, $6 seniors, $5 children (12–17). Free admission every Tuesday. Special exhibitions may have an extra charge.
GUIDED VISITS	Tours offered throughout the day. Audio tours available for $3, audio tours for special exhibits available for $5.
DISABLED ACCESS	From main entrance. Limited number of wheelchairs available at the museum. Audio tours for the visually impaired and printed scripts for the hearing impaired are available.
SERVICES	Museum store, café, coat check located on the (lower) terrace level
TELEPHONE	(415) 750-3600
WEB	www.thinker.org
MAIN ENTRANCE	Legion of Honor Drive in Lincoln Park, parking available without charge at the museum and along El Camino del Mar
GETTING THERE	Take bus #2 Clement to 34th St. or bus #18 46th Ave to the Legion (there is a $2 discount on museum entrance if you show your Muni transfer).

HIGHLIGHTS
Rodin Sculpture collection
Achenbach Collection of graphic arts
Peter Paul Rubens' *Tribute Money*
Oakes collection of Dutch, Flemish, and British paintings
Claude Monet's *Water Lilies*
Porcelain collection

The Palace of the Legion of Honor owes its building and the nucleus of its collection to Alma de Bretteville Spreckels and her husband, sugar magnate Adolph Spreckels, who commissioned the building in 1915. An avid art collector, Alma Spreckels' taste set the tone for the museum. Her collection of Rodin sculptures is one of the largest outside France, and her interest in French furniture, silver, ceramics, antiquities and objects of the theatre

Rembrandt Harmensz van Rijn *Joris de Caulerii* (1632)

and dance world is represented as well. The Legion's holdings have also been enriched by the gift of a significant collection of English and French porcelain, and by the Achenbach collection of graphic arts, the largest collection of works of art on paper in the western United States. In 1970, by uniting with the de Young Museum (see p. 101), the Legion gained the Oakes collection of Dutch, Flemish and British art from the 17th, 18th and 19th centuries.

THE BUILDING

At the Panama Pacific International Exposition of 1915, Alma de Brettville Spreckels' imagination was captured by the French Pavilion, a replica of the Palais de la Légion d'Honneur in Paris (1788). The French government granted her permission to build a permanent replica of the palace, set on a bluff overlooking the Pacific Ocean and the Golden Gate Bridge. Though World War I delayed construction, the museum (built to three-quarters scale) opened on Armistice Day in 1924 and was dedicated to the memory of the 3,600 men from California who died on the battlefields of France. A remodel and underground expansion in the early 1990s dramatically increased the square footage of the building without altering the historic beaux-arts façade.

Outside installations include the sculpture *Pax Jerusalemme* (1999) by **Mark di Suvero**, and the stark memorial *Holocaust* by **George Segal** (1984), which features a lone figure gazing through barbed wire to the ocean beyond.

THE COLLECTION

The Legion of Honor has two wings that branch out from a central rotunda, wrapping around the outdoor *Court of Honor*. For the most chronological tour, turn to your left from the rotunda and walk through *Gallery 6*, turning left again and passing through *Gallery 5* to *Gallery 1*.

Gallery 1 and 2 feature **MEDIEVAL ART**, roughly covering the 5th to the 15th C. It is interesting to compare the depiction of Mary

LEGION OF HONOR

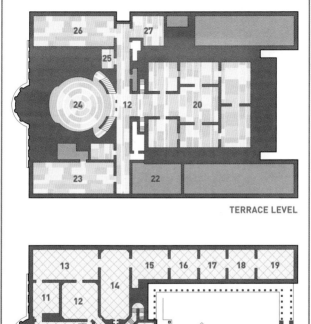

TERRACE LEVEL

Court of Honor

GROUND LEVEL

and baby Jesus in the *Adoration of the Magi* (1464-1510), by **Rodrigo de Osona the Elder**, with *Virgin and Child* (1460), by **Dieric Bouts** (or his studio). It's a thought-provoking example of painterly compromises—or not—between the portrayal of divinity and humanity in the subjects. As you enter *Gallery 3*, make sure to look up to see the 1490 ceiling from a palace in Toledo, Spain. The design of this three-ton wooden ceiling is filled with symbols, such as the scallop shells that signify the owners have made the pilgrimage to Santiago de Compostela in Spain.

Gallery 3 begins the display of **RENAISSANCE ART** with works from the 13th C on. Moving away from the Byzantine style of flat, iconic figures, the Renaissance emphasised the realistic rendering of figures. Artwork moved out of the churches, with the wealthy and aristocratic becoming arts patrons. In this room take note of the *Meeting of Sts Francis and Dominic* (1430) by **Fra Angelico**. Other notable works in the collection include *Madonna and Child* (1481) by **Bartolomeo Vivarini** and *Madonna Enthroned with Saints* (1466) by **Raffaellino del Garbo**. Compare these weighted figures with the flat rendering of *Sts Anthony and Stephen* (1373-1450) by **Bicci de Lorenzo**, also in this room. The *Last Judgement Triptych* (1500), painted by an unknown Tyrolean Master, shows the compressed space and flat gold background modelled on the Byzantine.

The Renaissance period peaked in the late 15th and early 16th C. The period before the Baroque age was characterised by **MANNERISM**, which focused on the technical execution of difficult human figures. This led to strained poses, unusual scale and often startling colour combinations. **El Greco**'s mystical paintings—note the elongated hands on his *St Peter* (1605-1610)—and **Potormo**'s *Madonna and Child with Two Angels* (1494-1557) (particularly in the long graceful neck, arms, and fingers of Mary) show Mannerist traits.

The artificiality of Mannerism caused a backlash, and, beginning with the 17th C, there developed a new style known for its vigorous emotionality. **BAROQUE ART** *(Gallery 6)* developed differently in different geographical areas—some exhibited an emphasis on dramatic colour and light, while other styles were subdued and classically inspired—though there was a consistent interest in study of the natural world and movement, with figures often portrayed mid-action. *St John the Baptist Preaching* (1665), by **Mattia Preti** (called Il Calabrese), is an example of Baroque painting's monumental scale, dynamic angles, and dramatic lighting effects, which all serve to draw the viewer into the image. **Georges de La Tour**'s twin portraits of *Old Man* and *Old Woman* show another use of dramatic Baroque lighting, as does the painting of *Young Boy Singing* (1620-40), by a French painter called the Candlelight Master.

The Baroque interest in the natural world extended to images of landscapes, such as *View of Tivoli at Sunset* (1642-44), by **Claude Gellée**, called Claude Lorraine, which shows the skyline of Rome on the horizon amongst the deepening shadows. The 17th C saw great increase in the popularity of landscapes and genre paintings such as *Peasants Before Their House* (1641) by **Louis Le Nain**.

Gallery 7 covers French and Italian art from the 18th C, the era of **ROCOCO** extravagance. Paris became the centre of the art world during this time. Artists such as **Jean-Antoine Watteau**, whose painting *Foursome* (1713) exemplifies the elegance and luxury enjoyed by the leisure classes, captures the subtle intimacy and sexual playfulness characteristic of the Rococo. Watteau's garden scenes, called *fêtes galantes*, were accepted into the French Academy in 1717.

Watteau had a tremendous influence on another Rococo master, **Francis Boucher**, whose mythological scenes, such as the *Companions of Diana* (1745) and *Bacchantes* (1745), also illustrate Rococo sensuousness. Boucher began his career as an engraver of Watteau's paintings, but rose to prominence under the patronage of Madame de Pompadour, mistress to Louis XV. In addition to painting, Boucher was the main designer for Sèvres porcelain and Beauvais tapestries, both pet projects of Pompadour.

One of Boucher's pupils, the painter **Jean-Honoré Fragonard**, is also known for paintings of mythology, landscape, and portraiture done for private patrons. Paintings such as *Useless Resistance* (1770) show a fluidity and sense of movement, as well as sexual overtones. Also in this room, note the four paintings by **Carle Vanloo**, which were shown in the Salon of 1753 to great acclaim. Vanloo, a rival of Boucher who was appointed first painter to the king by Louis XV in 1762, depicts children involved in artistic pursuits—painting, music, architecture, and sculpture.

Gallery 7 is also home to a number of examples of decorative furniture from this time period. The *French Cabinet on Stand* (1660) by Pierre Gole shows a level of elaborate decoration common to the Rococo. The *Sedan Chair* (1694-1752), which is attributed to Charles-Antoine Coypel, features gold gilding on the exterior.

For more 18th-C French decorative arts, continue to *Gallery 9a*. Here you will find a selection of colourful tapestries, gilded ceilings and walls, a dazzling chandelier, and examples of the elaborate furniture of the era. Take note of the inlaid table with pastoral scene attributed to Louis-Noëlle Malle (1765), a noted cabinetmaker during the reign of Louis XV.

Gallery 9a leads to *Gallery 9b*, where glassware is displayed. This display rotates, showing selections from the more than 400 vessels donated to the museum by Franz Sichel; the collection includes works from the 1st C to 1960. A small room off this gallery contains *Gallery 9c*, a decoratively painted chamber (France, 1680). There is often a sample of the museum's period clothing displayed here.

Gallery 10 could be considered the heart of the museum. It houses part of the large **RODIN SCULPTURE COLLECTION**, amassed by Alma Spreckels over a period of 35 years. One of the largest collection of **Auguste Rodin**'s work outside of France, it includes pieces in plaster and marble as well as bronze casts. Spreckels purchased many of the works directly from the artist.

Though in 1857 Rodin failed the entrance exam at the École des Beaux-Arts, he is now regarded as the most important sculptor of the 19th C and is credited with leading the way to Modernism by introducing emotional and psychological depth into the human figure. Inspired by the work of sculptors such as Michelangelo and Donatello, Rodin brought a strong knowledge of anatomy to his work—in fact, early critics assumed that he cast directly from a live model.

The focal point of *Gallery 10* is *Three Shades* (1880), figures created as part of the 'Gates of Hell' project planned for the doors to the Musée des Arts Décoratifs in Paris, a project upon which Rodin worked for over twenty years. Also in this room is the famous *Kiss* (1886), also conceived as part of the project. Rodin's work continues in *Gallery 8*. Keep an eye out for the *Burghers of Calais* (1906), considered to be amongst Rodin's finest work, and *Mighty Hand* (1906), a simple figure that illustrates the emotional power and expressiveness of Rodin's sculptures. Also note the small Rodin figures arranged in display cases along the corridor to the Rotunda, and from the Rotunda to *Gallery 12*.

Gallery 12 contains selections from the museum's sculpture collection.

In *Gallery 13* the focus changes from France to England, with **BRITISH PAINTING, FURNITURE AND SILVER** from the 18th and 19th C. The 1768 establishment of the Royal Academy of Arts under **Sir Joshua Reynolds** saw a resurgence in British art. Reynolds, who was appointed court painter to King George III in 1784, was influenced by the Baroque painters of the 17th C and by classical antiquities, the influence of which can be seen in his *Portrait of Anne, Viscountess, afterwards Marchioness of Townshend* (1780).

At that time another portrait painter, **Thomas Gainsborough** was—though he preferred landscape painting—in high demand. While Reynolds portraits tend towards the formal, Gainsborough portrayed his sitters in a more individual style. His portrait of *Mrs. Maria Anne Fitzherbert* (1784) shows the loose brushwork of Gainsborough's later work, and is an interesting comparison with the earlier portrait of *Samuel Kilderbee of Ipswich* (1755). Also of note is the *Landscape with Country Carts* (1784-5). This pastoral scene shows the influence of 17th-C Dutch landscapes, and forecast some of what was to come in the 19th C.

Also in *Gallery 13* is a display of furniture and English silver from the 1600-1800s. The *Bureau Cabinet* (1730), made of japanned wood, is particularly striking. For more furniture from this period make sure to visit *Gallery 11*, which contains a Neoclassical salon from the Hôtel d'Humières in Paris (1788). Amongst the furnishings in this salon is a sofa built for Marie Antoinette (1779) and cabinets filled with decorative pieces including Sèvres porcelain, French silver, music boxes, snuffboxes and German Meissenware.

Gallery 14 brings us to **DUTCH AND FLEMISH ART** of the 17th C. Religious and political differences during the 16th C had split the Low Countries into two nations; Catholic Flanders produced paintings that glorified the church, while painters in the Protestant Netherlands focused on genre scenes, landscapes, still lifes and portraits. The best-known painter of this period was the Flemish **Peter Paul Rubens**, considered the greatest artist of the Baroque era. His *Tribute Money* (1612) demonstrates the dramatic lighting and narrative power of his work. Rubens was highly sought after, serving as court painter in Italy and the Netherlands, and was knighted by both Charles I and Phillip IV. Not only successful as an artist, he undertook diplomatic missions to various European courts and helping to broker a peace treaty between England and Spain.

The Dutch painter **Rembrandt Harmensz van Rijn** was also developing a reputation during this time period, painting biblical and mythological scenes and portraits of the growing Dutch middle class. In the portrait of *Joris de Caulerii* (1632), the light that would fascinate the painter throughout his career is evident, but the portrait is rendered with a clarity and smoothness of style typical of Rembrandt's early work.

The 17th C in Holland saw the wide popularity of landscape and seascape paintings. **Jan van Goyen**'s *Thunderstorm* (1641) and **Salomon van Ruysdael**'s *River View of Nijmegen with the Valkhof* (1648) both show the low horizon line and large amount of sky typical of Dutch landscapes.

In addition to landscapes, still lifes imbued with Dutch Protestant values were also extremely popular in the Holland of the 17th C. Pocket watches symbolised life's fleeting nature, as did bouquets of flowers, often shown with petals dropping. Interrupted banquet scenes hinted at uncertainty or suggested moderation, while butterflies or dragonflies flapped their wings as rebirth—see the still life by **Abraham van Beyeren** (1666) in this gallery and the **Willem van Aelst** still life (1663) in *Gallery 15*, which continues with Dutch and Flemish portraits. **Frans Pourbus the Younger**'s *Portrait of a Lady* (1591) and *Portrait of a Gentleman in White* (1635) by **Frans Hals** make an interesting contrast of meticulous rendering and bravura brushwork. Hals was known for this sketchy brushwork, which became even looser as his career progressed. Both portraits demonstrate the increasing emphasis on the psychological portrayal of the sitter.

Also in this gallery is a landscape by the influential **Jacob van Ruisdael**, nephew of the Salomon van Ruysdael whose *River View* hangs in *Gallery 14*.

Gallery 16 covers the art of France in the 18th and 19th C, a turbulent period that saw the French Revolution, the rise of Napoleon, and the restoration of the Bourbon monarchy following Napoleon's defeat at Waterloo. As the revolution approached, the light-hearted and decorative style of the Rococo was left behind in favour of the more serious **NEOCLASSICISM**, which was also influenced by the discovery and excavation of ruins at Herculaneum and Pompeii in the 1730s and 1740s.

The master of Neoclassicism was **Jacques-Louis David**, a relative of the Rococo master Francis Boucher. David supported the Revolution and was active in the government, painting propagandistic revolutionary images. He almost lost his head after the fall of Robespierre, but regained a position of power under Napoleon, whose portraits and coronation scene he painted before fleeing France for Belgium when the monarchy was restored. The two David paintings in *Gallery 16* date from the later part of his career: the portrait of the artist's daughter, *Laure-Emilie-Felicite David, La Baronne Meunier* (1812), was painted shortly before his exile to Brussels, and the *Fortune Teller* (1824) was painted the year before his death. Both paintings seem unpolished (the portrait may be unfinished), unlike his earlier paintings, but the works still hint at David's skill as a colourist and his fine balance between realism and idealism.

Also in this gallery is the portrait of *La Comtesse de Morel-Vindé and her Daughter* (1799) painted by **Baron Francois-Pascal-**

Simon Gérard. Known for his portraits, Gérard was one of David's most accomplished students and received numerous commissions from Napoleon and Louis XVIII. There is also a portrait by **Elisabeth Louise Vigee Le Brun** (1755-1842), who began painting professionally while still a teenager. She was appointed court painter to Marie Antoinette, but fled France at the onset of revolution because of her royal connections. After twelve years of exile, Le Brun came back to France, after 255 artist colleagues successfully petitioned the government.

Gallery 17 contains 19th-C European art. It was a time of great change; painters in the **ROMANTIC** movement rebelled against Neoclassic restraint, preferring emotional intensity, subjective in nature, with an imaginative approach. This movement embraced a variety of painting styles, and melancholy, dramatic subject matters were common. Notable pictures include **Joseph Mallord William Turner**'s *View of Kenilworth Castle* (1830) and **Gustave Courbet**'s *Landscape in the Jura* (1864). Another painter who favoured landscapes was **Jean-Baptiste-Camille Corot**, whose *View of Rome* (1826-27) is the kind of painting that paved the way for Impressionism.

Another trend in the art of this period was an increased emphasis on realism. **Courbet** was the leader of this movement, and **Honoré Daumier**, whose *Third-Class Carriage* (1856-58) hangs in the gallery, was also a proponent. Best known during his lifetime as a social satirist—and jailed by Louis-Philippe for caricature and criticism of the king—Daumier became deeply interested in the lives of the underprivileged after working as a messenger boy for a bailiff in his early teens.

Also in this gallery are paintings by **Edouard Manet** and **Edgar Degas**, whose work laid the foundation for the **IMPRESSIONIST** movement. Manet's *Head of Christ* (1865) shows the loose handling of paint and contrast of light and dark characteristic of his work. Degas, a contemporary and friend of Manet's, helped organise the first Impressionist exhibit in 1874. His *Portrait of a Man* (1864) dates from the early part of his career, when he focused mainly on portraiture and classical composition. Degas was also known for his sculpture—keep an eye out for his

Trotting Horse, the Feet Not Touching the Ground (1881). He turned increasingly towards sculpture in his later years, as his eyesight began to fail.

Gallery 18 has paintings from the **VICTORIAN PERIOD**. In reaction to the formulaic compositions produced and praised by British Royal Academy of Art members, a group of young painters founded the Pre-Raphaelite Brotherhood (PRB) in 1848 in order to return to the realism and truth they felt could be found in art before the time of Raphael. **John Rodham Spencer-Stanhope** is considered to be of the second generation of pre-Raphaelite painters, and his *Love and the Maiden* (1829-1908) shows the theatrically romantic style associated with this later phase.

Thought not artistically a member of the Pre-Raphaelite Brotherhood, **Edward Lear**, whose landscape *Masada the Dead Sea* (1858) is displayed here, was friends with William Holman Hunt, one of the founding members. Lear, who briefly instructed Queen Victoria in drawing, was also known for his skill in illustration and was the author of numerous children's rhymes.

Also on display in this gallery are selections from the museum's collection of tapestries designed by **William Morris**. An accomplished designer, painter, furniture maker, stained-glass artist, writer and weaver, Morris spearheaded the Arts and Crafts Movement, a reaction against the increasing industrialisation of Britain during the 19th C.

Gallery 19 is the final gallery in this wing and is devoted to **IMPRESSIONIST & POST-IMPRESSIONIST ART**. Begun as a reaction to the French Academic painting styles, Impressionism had its roots in the realism of painters such as **Corot**. Named after an early **Claude Monet** painting titled *Impression: Sunrise*, the style sought to capture the visual experience of light and colour. Monet's *Grand Canal, Venice* (1908) shows the artist's fascination with atmosphere and the play of light, air and water. *Water Lilies* (1914–1917) is one of a series of paintings he did of the pond in his garden in Giverney, the painting of which occupied the last years of his life. **Pierre-Auguste Renoir**'s *Mother and Child* (1895) dates from the later part of his career, when he transitioned from Impressionism to a more weighty style of painting, influenced by the Italian Renaissance.

The Impressionist focus on visual experience caused some artists to venture in other directions. **Georges Pierre Seurat** was the founder of Neo-Impressionism, which attempted to find a more rational approach to describing light. His technique of pointillism—numerous dots of paint on white canvas—was rooted in the science of colour.

Paul Cézanne—though friends with many of the Impressionists and, like them, a believer of painting from nature—sought to bring some underlying structure to his paintings. In *Forest Interior* (1898-1899) it is possible to see the planes of colour and faceting that is characteristic of Cézanne's work. Cézanne is considered to be the father of modern art, and his work influenced many young artists. **Pablo Picasso**, whose painting, *Still Life with Skull, Leeks, and Pitcher* (1945), is in this gallery, considered Cézanne to be his one and only master.

TERRACE LEVEL

The lower level of the Legion of Honor contains the special exhibition areas, as well as the museum's collection of porcelain and antiquities. The terrace level can be reached via staircases that branch off on either side of the central rotunda. There is handicapped access via lifts in *Galleries 5 and 15*.

To continue with the permanent collection, turn away from the special collections once you reach the bottom of the stairs and turn left at the theatre entrance. At the end of this corridor, you will find the *Constance and Henry Bowles Porcelain Gallery*, named after the husband and wife collectors who began donating their collection of **ENGLISH AND FRENCH PORCELAIN** to the museum in the 1980s. The Bowles collection is extensive, featuring porcelain from Sèvres, Capodimonte, Meissen, Mennecy, Worcester, Chelsea and Longton Hall, and was a significant addition to the museum's ceramics collection. Make sure to note the playful German Meissen figurines (18th-19th C), and the *English Dovecote Perfume Burner* (1755-1756), from the Chelsea

Factory. Also, the *Covered Dish in Shape of Dormouse* (1760), from Jingdezhen China, a gift to the museum from Alma Spreckels, is worth tracking down for its playful whimsy.

In the corridor outside the porcelain gallery, the museum's collection of **ANTIQUITIES** is displayed, including Greek and Italian pottery and figures in terracotta, limestone, marble and bronze. Note the red-figure pottery from Greece (6th C BC), which features striking red figures on a black background. Many of these vases would have been buried in tombs, filled with wine and other foodstuffs, as gifts for the dead. Being entombed protected the vases, and the designs on the exterior reveal much about the culture and mythology of Greece during this time period.

There are also several Etruscan pieces. The Etruscans reigned in Italy beginning in the 8th century BC, and even the Greeks prized their metal work. Note the Etruscan black-glaze pottery from southern Italy (4th C BC), as well as the bronze *Statuette of a Reclining Banqueter* (6th C BC).

Several pieces in this collection were given to Alma de Brettville Spreckels by Queen Elizabeth of Greece, as gifts for the museum. Note the terracotta *Hippocamp* (3rd C BC), the Cypriot *Bull Askos* (1400-1230 BC), and the *Archaic Female Figure* (6th C BC).

The second part of the corridor, past the theatre, features Assyrian, Syro-Phoenician, Syrian and Egyptian objects. The *Relief from the Tomb of Mentuemhet* (660 BC) features colourful illustrations on limestone, while the *Torso of a God* (1363-1353 BC) has lost an arm and head but still shows the classic stylistic details of Egyptian statues. The playful *Anatolian Lion-Shaped Rhyton* (1860-1780 BC) was another gift from the Greek Queen.

Also off this corridor is the display room for the *Reva and David Logan Collection of Illustrated Books*. One of the most important collections of artists' books (livres d'artistes), the collection features original prints and notes by artists such as **Fernand Léger**, **Henri de Toulouse-Lautrec**, **Edouard Manet** and **Pablo Picasso**. The collection spans over 100 years, from 1870-2000, and represents nearly every art movement of the 20th C. The collection room features a rotating selection of books according to artist or theme.

in the area

The Presidio In this space were planted the seeds of modern San Francisco. Spanish colonial forces set up their *presidio*, or garrison, on this northwestern corner of the peninsula in 1776. The base was inherited by Mexico in 1822 and occupied by the Americans in 1846. As the United States came of age as a Pacific power, the Presidio's significance grew; during the Spanish-American War, the base was a staging ground for troops headed to the Philippines. The military installation became a national park in 1994 and now boasts hiking and biking trails, a golf course, meadows, forests, a beach and gorgeous oceanside views—which all feel a million miles away from the city. The Presidio's history is still very much in evidence, though: barracks and officer's quarters still line the streets. **Map p. 127, 3A**

Fort Point Open 10 am–5 pm, Fri–Sun (during Golden Gate Bridge seismic retrofitting). Once thought impregnable, this austere brick fortress actually became obsolete soon after it opened in 1861. For nearly a century, Fort Point protected San Francisco Bay from threats—Confederate ships, enemy subs— that never came. Today the building is literally overshadowed by the Golden Gate Bridge, but this elderly veteran has weathered the indignities of age and history with good grace. Fort Point has been preserved as an example of a 19th-C coastal fortification. There are gorgeous views of the Golden Gate on the approach to the fort. Interesting exhibits inside reveal the fort's sturdy design, the layout of its defences and give a taste of the life its soldiers lived. **Off map**

The Golden Gate Bridge Southbound auto toll $5. This Art Deco span has become synonymous with San Francisco. The Bay Bridge is longer and carries more traffic, but the Golden Gate's sleek design and unmistakable hue make it an eternal favourite. 'International orange' paint was chosen to make the bridge stand out in the fog, as well as to harmonise with the reddish-brown Marin headlands. Despite the difficulty of building the foundations,

An icon: the Golden Gate Bridge, opened 1937

the bridge's builders sustained relatively few casualties on the job. Since the bridge opened in 1937, far more have died as suicides, for whom it has an irresistable draw. You can walk onto the bridge (or even across, if you're in the mood). **Off map**

Lincoln Park Canopied by cypress and eucalyptus trees, Lincoln Park offers hikers and bikers remarkable vistas of the Golden Gate and the Marin headlands on the far shore. Vestiges of a grand past still haunt the coast here. Today's Cliff House, a restaurant with gorgeous oceanside views, stands on the site of a titanic Victorian structure that burned to the ground. Concrete foundations are all that remains of the once-mighty Sutro Baths, a pool complex built in 1886 that could hold more than 10,000 swimmers. At low tide three shipwrecks from the 1920s and 1930s emerge from the waters northeast of Point Lobos—testimony to the treacherous fog. For the east side of the park, take the #1 or 2 bus; for the Cliff House and the coast, take the #18 or 38. **Map p. 126, 1-3A to 1-3B**

eat

$ **Angkor Wat** 4217 Geary Blvd., (415) 221-7887. 11 am–2.30 pm, Mon–Sat; 5 pm–10 pm, Sun. The plush sunken tables in the centre of the colourful room seem perfect as you nestle down and prepare for an evening's indulgence. The Cambodian menu, well-spiced and highly aromatic, includes lemongrass curries made with citronelle and garlic. River fish are spiced with chilli and basil, and aubergine is heavy with garlic. A coconut custard steamed in banana leaf (*Amok*) is good for those who like it mild. **Map p. 127, 2C** ❶

Burma Superstar 309 Clement St., (415) 387-2147. 11 am–9.30 pm, Tue–Sun. Easy to spot in the dark for the golden light pouring through the storefront window. Inside it's tightly packed with happy people tucking into a wide range of colourful and spicy Burmese dishes. Rich and creamy curries sing in the mouth but don't quite burn, and vegetables are seasoned just enough to bring them to life. A rare treat is '*la pet*,' a fresh green tea salad tossed with sesame and lime. **Map p. 127, 3B** ②

Java Source 343 Clement St., (415) 387-8025. Open 7 am–11 pm. The dark wood furniture and the deep, narrow dimensions of the room give this coffee house a bohemian feel. Popular with locals as a place to read the newspaper, sip one of the many coffees or teas, or just relax as the world goes by. The house also offers freshly made crêpes with a variety of fillings both sweet and savoury. Smokers will be glad to know the patio is theirs. **Map p. 127, 3B** ③

Plough and Stars 116 Clement St., between 2nd and 3rd, (415) 751-1122. Open 4 pm–2 am, Mon; 2 pm–2 am, Tue–Thur; 12 pm–2 am, Fri–Sun. A very traditional Irish pub, and a good place to crawl to after dinner in a nearby restaurant. The main furnishings are long wooden tables and many, many barstools. Irish (and other) poets read from their works here. Travelling (and local) musicians perform fairly regularly. And when the Guinness is flowing, patrons are likely to spontaneously break into song. **Map p. 127, 3B** ④

Taiwan Restaurant 445 Clement St., (415) 387-1789. 11 am–10 pm, Sun–Thur; 11 am–12 am, Sat. A rather old establishment, and a bit threadbare in places, but it's as comfortable as an old shoe, and smells a lot better. The specialities of the glassed-in kitchen are noodles, wontons and pot stickers, which you'll see being made by hand as you enter. The most popular dishes are the noodle soups, especially the 'beef soup noodles with own gravy'. At lunch time the rice plates ($3.50) make for one of the cheapest meals in town. **Map p. 127, 2B** ⑤

$$ **Clement Street Bar and Grill** 708 Clement St., (415) 386-2200. Lunch: 11.30 am–2 pm, Tue–Sat. Dinner: 5.30 pm–10 pm, Tue–Sat; 4.30 pm–9.30 pm, Sun. Brunch: 10.30 am–3 pm, Sat and Sun. A ship's cabin atmosphere with much dark wood and brass. The entrance is dominated by the ample bar while a great red brick fireplace warms the spacious dining room. The Italian-inspired menu features roasted garlic with crostini; roasted red pepper with three cheeses; and spinach salad with herbs and pine nuts for starters. Veal scaloppini, grilled Portobello mushroom, and wild mushroom tortellini with roma tomatoes are popular main dishes. **Map p. 127, 2B** ⑥

Pizza Orgasmica 823 Clement St., (415) 386-6000. 11 am–12 am. Plush cushions on the floor under a pavilion, luxurious booths by the fire, a mural of the temptation of Eve in the bar...is this a pizzeria or a brothel? Try the 'Ménage à Trois' pizza with three cheeses, and for something sinful the pungent garlic 'Serpent's Kiss' will lead you off the straight and narrow. Vegetarians will enjoy the 'Kama Sutra'. **Map p. 127, 2B** 7

$$$ **Clementine** 126 Clement St., (415) 387-0408. Step into this room and be transported to a French provincial town. Copper pans and oil paintings grace the peach walls, while the skilful use of soft light and mirrors suffuses the room with a delicious cosiness. Classic French dishes are what you come here for: rack of lamb with gratin Dauphinois; Coquille Saint-Jacques with Savoy cabbage braised in mussel juice; confit of duck; or a simple veal chop. Service is attentive and highly polished. **Map p. 127, 3B** 8

shop

CLOTHES

April in Paris 55 Clement St., (415) 750-9910, www.aprilinparis.us. More than just a leather shop. Artisan Beatrice Amblard will make custom leather goods at the workshop inside this boutique. High-end handbags, belts, wallets and watchbands are just some of the items she works, but handbags are the main draw; they take six months and can cost from $1,600 up. The shop also carries a small selection of Suzanne George one-of-a-kind dress shoes. **Map p. 127, 3B** 1

Brands Off 6 Clement St., (415) 831-8880, www.brands-off.com. They don't shun brands, really—the name of this shop is taken from a Japanese magazine. Colourful, Italian-made handbags are the focus, with designs from Francesco Biasia, Gianna Z, Meanilli and Belmira Dorego, to name a few. Bags come in all colours and fabrics, and there is a small selection of pre-owned bags at lower prices, including Gucci, Prada and Vivian Westwood. It also offers a 50%-off sale rack. **Map p. 127, 3B** 2

A Mary Frances bag at Brands Off

Fashion Exchange 533 Clement St., (415) 933-0078. Brand-name new and used clothing at wholesale prices. While much of the stock is casual wear, it is possible to find Theory, BCBG and Cache formal dresses, as well. Fashion Exchange also carries accessories like good shoes and inexpensive jewellery. **Map p. 127, 2B** ❸

Fashion Pulse 440 Clement St., (415) 831-2618. Though this store doesn't exactly keep its pulse on high fashion, it does offer modern styles at low prices. The store carries a range of women's designs, including casual dresses, skirts, outerwear and quality sweaters. For the prices, it's possible to do quite a bit of shopping without encountering the guilt factor. **Map p. 127, 2B** ❹

Get Thee to a Nunnery 908 Clement St., (415) 752-8889. Despite the name of this shop, Get Thee to a Nunnery has been bringing a dash of sophistication to the bargain basement Richmond District for more than 20 years. There are two floors full of high-quality clothes, most made of natural fibres. The quality of the clothes is miles above many of the other local shops, but the prices here are actually very reasonable. **Map p. 127, 2B** ❺

Go Figure 124 Clement St., (415) 876-4924, www.gofiguresf.com. The motto at this plus-size store is 'Clothes for women of generous proportions'. Using mostly Californian and Canadian designers, the casual clothes at this relaxed shop are made from linen, rayon and silks. Go Figure also specialises in clothes for the mother of the bride. **Map p. 127, 3B** ❻

Satin Moon Fabrics 32 Clement St., (415) 668-1623. Satin Moon squeezes fabrics from all over the world into its compact space. Some of the more exotic fabrics include Japanese silk, embroidered silk from India and fine Italian wools. Though fabrics can be used for clothing, most of the business at this shop is in decorating and upholstery. The shop does referrals to dressmakers, upholsterers and drapery designers, and also sells a wide selection of decorating trim for pillows, bedspreads, curtains. Closed Sundays and Mondays. **Map p. 127, 3B** ②

Kimberley's Consignment Shoppe 3020 Clement St., (415) 752-2223. Not your run-of-the-mill used-clothing shop! The attraction is low prices for these big-name labels. There are many high-end designer labels in stock, such as Prada, Gucci and Versace, and most are in excellent shape. Kimberley's carries both men's and women's clothes, and has excellent service. **Map p. 126, 3B** ⑦

GIFTS

The Hobby Company 5150 Geary Blvd., (415) 386-2802. This expansive store carries supplies for just about any craft hobbyist or school project. Merchandise is organised in different sections, with models, kites, glue and other tools to put the items together. The needlework area includes fabric, needles and thread, while the crafts section features silk flowers, rubber stamps, and wooden boxes. The store also carries beads and doll's houses, as well as books on arts and crafts. **Map p. 127, 1C** ⑧

Regina 5845 Geary Blvd., (415) 386-8577. Much of the inventory at this shop is imported from Russia. One of the main gift items available is the line of traditional Matryoshka dolls, or wooden, hand-painted nesting dolls that stack inside each other to represent the generations of a family. Regina also offers china, lacquer boxes and jewellery, including lots of amber. **Map p. 126, 4C** ⑨

Smile Gifts 544 Clement St., (415) 668-9968. Hello Kitty takes centre stage at this tiny gift shop. The feline is branded on everything imaginable—shower curtains, toothbrush sets, alarm clocks, blankets notebooks. Aside from the Hello Kitty paraphernalia, Smile also carries Monchhichi dolls and Yu-Gi-Oh figures. **Map p. 127, 2B** ③

Torgsyn 5542 Geary Blvd., (415) 752-5546. Torgsyn primarily sells antique and estate jewellery. The friendly neighbourhood shop also sells glass and china for the home and a collection of clocks. The staff is quite knowledgeable. **Map p. 127, 1C** ⑩

BOOKS

Green Apple Books & Music 506 Clement St., (415) 387-2272; annex at 520 Clement St., www.greenapplebooks.com. Considered by locals to be one of San Francisco's best bookshops, Green Apple has been offering new and used books for more than 30 years. The main location has two floors filled with standard hardback and paperback titles, an overwhelming selection of remainders and used books, and new and used CDs. Sections cover every category possible, from metaphysics to feminist theory. The annex on the same block features books on tape, DVDs and the genre fiction collection. **Map p. 127, 2B** ❸

Thidwick Books 11 Clement St., (415) 831-1600. This small independent neighbourhood bookstore carries a wide selection on its colourful shelves. What is purposefully left out are spiritual or New Age books, as well as business or computer titles. Also for sale are fun items like finger puppets, magnets and artistic greeting cards journals. A bulletin board of humorous cartoons cut from various newspapers sets the tone at Thidwick. **Map p. 127, 3B** ❷

KIDS

Cards & Comics Central 5424 Geary Blvd., (415) 668-3544. Sports trading cards, especially baseball and basketball cards, are all the rage at this collectibles shop. Cards & Comics also placates the needs of comics buffs with its array of mainstream comic books. **Map p. 127, 1C** ⓫

Citikids 152 Clement St., (415) 752-3837, www.citikids.com. The tagline for Citikids is 'The complete children's store'. Considering the size of the store, that can't help but be the case. Offering the largest selection of baby goods in San Francisco, this spot is really one-stop shopping for everything from car seats and strollers to bottles and bibs. The department store also offers baby-proofing gear and clothes for infants and toddlers. **Map p. 127, 3B** ❻

shop!

Henry's Entertainment 5442 Geary Blvd., (415) 831-8123. Henry's Entertainment specialises in Japanese manga, with figurines, trading cards and other pop culture toys. The shop also offers a small selection of old Beanie Babies. **Map p. 127, 1C** ❿

Heroes Club 840 Clement St., (415) 387-4552, www.artoftoy.com. Renowned throughout the Bay Area for its Japanese import figures and collectibles, Heroes Club also taps heavily into the world of action figures, urban vinyl and collector's cards. Another Heroes speciality is rare stuff like the Chogokin Chronicle book. **Map p. 127, 2B** ❺

Jean et Marie 100 Clement St., (415) 379-1111, www.jeanetmarie.com. Parents interested in keeping their kids in high fashion can find a selection of French import baby and children's clothes at this boutique. Catering to newborns up to kids age 8, Jean et Marie carries Petit Bateau and Catimini, and toys from Corolle, Kalloo and Vilac. **Map p. 127, 3B** ❶

HOME

Gaslight & Shadows 2335 Clement St., (415) 387-0633. Gaslight & Shadows is known for its large collection of Limoges porcelain boxes. The styles vary but each of the dainty boxes is heavily detailed. Aside from the box collection, Gaslight also sells antique watches, ceramics, lamps and an assortment of fine quality as well as inexpensive costume jewellery. **Map p. 126, 4B** 12

Kamei House Wares & Restaurant Supply 525–547 Clement St., (415) 666-3688. Leave plenty of time to scan the shelves at this massive shop. Kamei offers sake sets, tea sets, mini rice cookers, chopsticks, storage containers and everything else for the home, all at excellent prices. **Map p. 127, 2B** 3

Kumquat Art & Home Accessories 9 Clement St., (415) 752-2140, www.kumquatart.com. A true potpourri of goods awaits inside Kumquat. Owner Keverne Tuomey carries crafts and other products produced by Bay Area or California individuals or companies, steering clear of mass-market items. Her stock runs the gamut from recycled rubber coasters to hand-painted ceramic candleholders. A wall of affordable paintings by local artists rotates every couple of months. **Map p. 127, 3B** 2

Muzzy's Attic 3448 Balboa St., (415) 831-4338. Sifting through the two floors of consignment items at Muzzy's Attic is like spending an afternoon at a good garage sale. The prices are bottom line, and the store even marks down some things, making shopping there still cheaper. **Map p. 126, 3C** 13

Period George 7 Clement St., (415) 752-1900, www.periodgeorge.com. Store owner Donald Gibson wants table settings to be as carefully and artfully thought out as the food that's on the plates. Period George carries mostly antique dishes, glasse, and silverware. Much of the exquisite stock comes from overseas and can be sold as sets or separates, making some of the finer, expensive pieces more financially accessible. **Map p. 127, 3B** 2

MISCELLANEOUS

Bargain Bank 599 Clement St., (415) 221-4852. Though Bargain Bank looks like it's perpetually in clearance mode, with its random displays and somewhat dishevelled interior, this shop is worth a visit. Much of the merchandise comes from overstock at other stores or is leftovers from shops going out of business. Bargains can be had for everything from fine wines to Wallace & Gromet videos. The motto here is 'Why Pay More?' **Map p. 127, 2B** 3

Vinh Khang Herb & Ginseng 512 Clement St., (415) 752-8336. This small shop is packed with hundreds of drawers full of herbs. The shop's claim to fame came when actress Julia Roberts filmed here in *Dying Young*. This shop has become popular via word of mouth. **Map p. 127, 2B** ❸

Enter Pacific 843 Clement St., (415) 386-1388. Geared toward the Asian population of the district. One whole area of the store is dedicated to CDs, DVDs and videos, mostly from Hong Kong and mainland China. Gift items include Pucca, Monchhichi and Pokemon paraphernalia. **Map p. 127, 2B** ❺

The Marina & Cow Hollow

The Marina may be one of the more culturally homogeneous areas of San Francisco, but it also harbours some of the most eclectic shopping. Dairy farming was once the mainstay of Cow Hollow; now *Union St.* is full of designer boutiques and upscale chain stores. It's also packed with pricey jewellery shops, high-end children's clothing and toy stores, and home furnishing shops.

Most locals prefer the less ritzy stores along *Chestnut St.*, between Fillmore and Baker. Chestnut features several body shops, spas and salons, as well as women's boutiques, accessories shops, and neighbourhood grocers and florists.

There are a few standout clothing shops in the area. **Bryan Lee** (1840 Union St.) is revered for its personal service. The emphasis for both men and women is finding each individual's exact fit and right look. **Porto** (1770 Union St.) is a find for women who love Italian clothes, while **Giggle** (2110 Chestnut St., www.egiggle.com) aims to be one-stop shopping for parents, with an emphasis on healthy, natural, chemical-free products. Toys are made from naturally finished wood and washable fabrics.

Riley James (3027 Fillmore St.) spans two floors. Clothes upstairs range from casual to upscale, with labels like Punk Royal, J. Lindeberg, Lamb, and See By Chloe, as well as hip

shop

and offbeat shoes by Hollywould. The men's section has a game room in back with old-school arcade games, poker nights and a wireless PlayStation.

American crafts store **Twig** (2162 Union St., twigcrafts.com) stands as one of the more funky, whimsical shops on Union St.—they showcase a 'martini glass of the month'. And when it comes down to shoes, **Shaw** (2001 Union St., www.shawshoes.net) is the spot. For more than 34 years, Shaw has been celebrating women's feet with a dizzying array of high-end Italian shoes with playful designs, such as pink leopard-spot boots and butterfly-adorned sandals.

One of the highlights of any day of Marina shopping is a stop at **Gity Joon** (1828 Union St., www.gityjoon.com). No less than 41 countries are represented at this home decor and gift shop. Don't leave without seeing the divine 108-piece, hand-painted, 24-karat gold leaf, 18th-C royal wedding bed from China.

shop'

entertainment

INFORMATION
TICKETS
VENUES
NIGHTLIFE
TOURS
FESTIVALS

INFORMATION

San Francisco harbours one of the most diverse arts and culture scenes in the country, with a multitude of live music venues, dance clubs, independent movie theatres, lively bars and travelling shows

The free weekly papers, *SF Weekly* and the *Bay Guardian*, are the best sources for live-music information, as is *The Wave*, and the 'Pink Section' of the *San Francisco Chronicle*'s Sunday edition.

VENUES

When it comes to performance space, San Francisco is home to a number of glorious concert halls and refurbished old theatres.

CLASSICAL

San Francisco Symphony at the Louise M. Davies Symphony Hall 210 Van Ness Ave., (415) 864-6000. The San Francisco Symphony gave its first concert in 1911, and has been one of the country's top symphonies since. Under the direction of Michael Tilson Thomas, the orchestra has won a number of prestigious recording awards. Performances take place at the exquisite Davies Hall, which is open for tours during the week. **Map p. 76, 3-4B**

San Francisco Opera at the War Memorial Opera House 301 Van Ness Ave., (415) 864-3330 (tickets), (415) 861-4008 (general info), (510) 524-5220 (tours). The War Memorial Opera House has gilded chandeliers, an orchestra pit on hydraulic lifts and other lavish touches. **Map p. 76, 3-4B**

San Francisco Ballet at the War Memorial Opera House 301 Van Ness Ave., (415) 865-2000. Distinguished as the oldest professional ballet company in the country, the San Francisco Ballet was founded in 1933 as the San Francisco Opera Ballet. The company came close to folding in the mid-1970s, but community support helped save it, and today it is one of the largest and most important ballet companies in the US. **Map p. 76, 3-4B**

CONTEMPORARY

San Francisco is certainly a city of rock, with a lively history—everyone from Chubby Checker to the Sex Pistols played here—and a vibrant live music scene. The city's largest venues include the **Bill Graham Civic Auditorium** (99 Grove St., (415) 974-4000), a four-story Beaux-Arts building for mega-concerts; **Cow Palace** (Geneva Ave. and Santos St., (415) 404-4111), which hosts expos, parties, and occasional concerts; and the **Avalon Ballroom** (1268 Sutter St., (415) 252-7100), where the likes of Janis Joplin used to play. **The Grand** (1300 Van Ness Ave., (415) 673-5716) also hosts some of the larger names, while **StudioZ.tv** (314 11th St., (415) 252-7666) accommodates live acts and large parties.

The Fillmore 1805 Geary at Fillmore, (415) 346-6000. The Fillmore is San Francisco's most historic music venue. It first opened in 1912 as a dance hall, and later became renowned for hosting just about every legendary act of the 1960s. Upstairs, the walls are filled with posters from hundreds of Fillmore shows. **Map p. 76, 1A**

The Warfield 982 Market St., (415) 775-7722. This ornate hall opened in 1922. The floor slopes and there is an upper balcony, making it easy to get a decent view even at the most crowded of shows. **Map p. 8, 1C**

The Great American Music Hall 859 O'Farrell St., (415) 861-8900. Another legendary music spot. It was built in 1907 and was a popular restaurant and bordello under the name Blanco's until 1933. The hall still has marble columns, ceiling frescoes and an ornate balcony. **Map p. 76, 4A**

Bimbo's 365 Club 1025 Columbus Ave., (415) 474-0365. It first opened as a speakeasy in 1931 and became a supper club after the end of Prohibition. The plush decor—red carpet and velvet curtained stage—still evokes a big band feel, though the live acts that perform here are much more eclectic, ranging from contemporary blues to alternative rock. **Map p. 39, 2B**

Café du Nord 2170 Market St., (415) 861-5016. Another old speakeasy, this one built in 1907. It reopened in 1991 as part of the 1990s swing revival. The décor from its early days has not changed much—heavy red velvet curtains, a carved mahogany bar, red pool table and candlelit tables. The live music now includes jazz, swing, alternative rock, hip-hop and spoken word. **Map p. 52, 2A**

Slim's 333 11th St., (415) 255-0333. One of the city's premiere clubs for rock, blues, and roots music, opened in 1988 by R&B artist Boz Scaggs. **Off map**

Other main live venues include the **Independent** (628 Divisadero St., (415) 771-1421), the **Bottom of the Hill** (1233 17th St., (415) 621-4455), and the **DNA Lounge** (375 11th St., (415) 626-1409). For jazz, the best outlet requires a ride across the Bay to **Yoshi's** (510 Embarcadero West, Jack London Square, Oakland, 510-238-9200).

THEATRE

The centre of San Francisco's theatre district lies within the Union Square region (Map p. 8, 2A). Some of the travelling Broadway shows stop here, but many of the performances at these theatres are original scripts. The city's main theatres include the **Curran Theater** (445 Geary St., (415) 776-1999), the **Golden Gate Theatre** (1 Taylor St, (415) 551-2000), the **Geary Theatre** (415 Geary, (415) 749-2228)—home to the prestigious **American Conservatory Theatre**—and the **Lorraine Hansberry Theatre** (620 Sutter St, (415) 474-8800.)

Of course there's more to performance than theatre. The **Herbst Theatre at Civic Center** (401 Van Ness Avenue, (415) 392-4400, Map p. 76, 3-4B) features the City Arts and Lecture Series as well as spoken word, solo musical performances, and other theatrical events. Located in the city's historic Cannery Building, **Cobb's Comedy Club** (2801 Leavenworth, (415) 928-4320, Map p. 39, 1A) has been the main comedy venue in the city for more than 20 years. There are comedy performances nightly and two shows on Fri and Sat nights.

The kitschy cabaret show Beach Blanket Babylon has become a permanent feature in San Francisco's entertainment scene. The musical is loosely based on the story of Snow White travelling the world to find her prince, along the way encountering a cast of 'stars' portrayed by the wacky cast in outlandish costumes. The show runs at **Club Fugazi** (678 Green St., at Powell, (415) 421-4222, Map p. 8, 1A).

NIGHTLIFE

Though it's not as sleepless as New York, San Francisco does have a spirited nightlife, with dance music and DJs at the heart of the scene.

The highest concentration of bars and nightclubs is in SOMA (Map p. 8, 3B-C). The **EndUp** (401 Sixth St., (415) 357-0827) draws a large gay crowd, though the club is very open to people of all sexual orientations. Fag Fridays is always a big party, as is the after-hours T Dance all day Sunday, featuring deep house music. **1015 Folsom** (1015 Folsom St.,

The Geary Theatre

(415) 431-1200), one of the largest dance clubs in the city, features house, trance, techno, and drum 'n' bass DJs every weekend. The three-level club also hosts top international DJs, as well as live acts on the centre level's main stage. The unpretentious down and dirty **Club Six** (60 6th St., (415) 531-6593) also features an eclectic mix.

AsiaSF (201 Ninth St., (415) 255-2742) takes the concept of dinner theatre to another realm. Elegant drag queens are the entertainment as well as the wait staff. The bar has an extensive sake and sake cocktail selection, which can be enjoyed while watching lip-synch performances by 'gender illusionists'.

DJs help fill the massive dance floor at the trendy **Mezzanine** (444 Jessie St., (415) 625-8880), and also bring in the crowds to the hip cocktail lounge **Wish** (1539 Folsom St., (415) 278-9474). **111 Minna Gallery** (111 Minna St., (415) 974-1719) splits time as a cutting-edge gallery by day and a jam-packed club by night. A couple of good pre-club stops include the space-age **Café Mars** (798 Brannan St., (415) 621-6277) and the pub-style, rockin' **Hotel Utah Saloon** (500 4th St., 415) 546-6300.)

In **UNION SQUARE** (Map p. 8, 2B), the highlight is the Latin jazz lounge **Azul** (1 Tillman Pl., (415) 362-9750), while **Sublounge** (628 20th St., (415) 552-3603) in China Basin, decorated in retro-aeroplane style, has become one of the most popular DJ bars in the city.

NORTH BEACH (Map p. 39, 2-3B) is the spot for outdoor cafés and late-evening people-watching at popular spots like **Tosca** (242 Columbus Ave., (415) 986-9651) and **Vesuvio Café** (255 Columbus Ave.; (415) 362-3370). The best Marina hangout is **MatrixFillmore** (3138 Fillmore St., (415) 563-4180), originally the Matrix Club when it was opened in 1965 by Marty Balin, lead singer for the Jefferson Airplane. The club now features DJs every night, playing a variety of groove and lounge music.

Another hip nightlife area is the **MISSION DISTRICT** (Map p. 52, 3-4C-D). The **Elbo Room** (647 Valencia St., (415) 552-7788), is a bar with a range of music genres. Bars like the **Casanova Lounge** (527 Valencia St., (415) 863-9328), **Beauty Bar** (2299 Mission St., (415) 285-0323) and **Dalva** (3121 16th St., (415) 252-7740) are local hangouts during the week and crowded with bridge and tunnel crowds at the weekends. The **Make-Out Room** (3225 22nd St., (415) 647-2888) and **12 Galaxies** (2565 Mission St., 415) 970-9777) are popular with locals for their live music. **Levende Lounge** (1710 Mission St., 415) 864-5585) draws locals for its smooth grooves and tasty cocktails. A unique Mission bar is the **Oxygen Bar Sushi & Sake Lounge** (795 Valencia St., (415) 255-2102), where patrons inhale oxygen while relaxing on couches.

The **OUTER MISSION** (Map p. 52, 3-4D) is home to some eclectic bars and clubs, such as **El Rio** (3158 Mission St., (415) 282-3325), known for its Sunday afternoon salsa parties, and **26 Mix** (3024 Mission St., (415) 826-7378), known for its superb DJs. The **Odeon Bar** (3223 Mission St, 415) 550-6994) is one of the quirkiest and craziest bars in town.

The **LOWER HAIGHT** (Map p. 100, 4B-C) features a few good and gritty bars and clubs such as **Noc Noc** (557 Haight St., (415) 861-5811) and **Nickie's BBQ** (460 Haight St, (415) 621-6508), which is always packed for its weekend funk dance parties.

The **CASTRO** (Map p. 52, 1A), which has the largest concentration of gay bars and clubs in the city, is also the liveliest section of town. The colourful crowds head to the **Café** (2367 Market St., 415) 861-3846), the **Lexington Club** (3464 19th St., (415) 863-2052) and the laid-back **Martuni's** (4 Valencia St., (415) 241-0205), to name a few.

There are several bars around the city frequented largely by tourists, but for good reason. **Harry Denton's Starlight Room** (450 Powell St., on the 21st floor of the Sir Frances Drake Hotel, (415) 395-8595) draws an upscale crowd of swanky drink sippers, and offers some of the best views of downtown San Francisco. **Hurricane Bar** (950 Mason St., (415) 772-5278) in the Fairmont Hotel's **Tonga Room**, serves the best happy hour in San Francisco. **Top of the Mark** (Number One Nob Hill, (415) 392 3434), set on the top floor of the Mark Hopkins hotel on Nob Hill, boasts 360-degree views from any table in the room. Some locals come for the live music Thur–Sat. Built in the 1890s, **Ruby Skye** (420 Mason St., (415) 693-0777), an old Victorian Playhouse, features local and international DJs. Since opening in the 1890s, the **Buena Vista Café** (2765 Hyde St., (415) 474-5044) has become renowned for its Irish coffee, serving an average of 2,000 glasses a day. Buena Vista is the perfect resting spot for those visiting Fisherman's Wharf (Map p. 39, 1-2A), and an Irish coffee the perfect elixir for those cold, foggy nights.

CINEMA

With all the film festivals and independent movie houses in San Francisco, the city's film scene is definitely alive and well.

Castro Theatre 429 Castro St., (415) 621-6120. This is by far the most regal movie house in the city (see p. 57). The centrepiece of the Castro Theatre is the mighty Wurlitzer organ, which is still played before movies and as accompaniment to silent films. The Castro screens classic and art films, and is home to the San Francisco International Film Festival. **Map p. 52, 1B**

The Roxie 3117 16th St. (415) 863-1087 The Roxie has carved a niche as a venue for independent films, documentaries, B-movies, and other rarities. **Map p. 52, 3A-B**

The Red Vic 1727 Haight St., (415) 668-3994. This scruffy-yet-comfy theatre (with couches) shows indie films and second-run flicks. **Map p. 100, 3B**

Foreign Cinema screens foreign movies outdoors for you to watch while you have dinner. See p. 63.

Almost any time of year, a film festival is sure to be going on.

February	The San Francisco Independent Film Festival
March	NAATA's San Francisco International Asian American Film Festival
April	The San Francisco International Film Festival (the oldest in the country)
June	The San Francisco Black Film Festival and The San Francisco International Lesbian and Gay Film Festival
July	The San Francisco Jewish Film Festival
October	Cinemayaat: The Arab Film Festival
November	American Indian Film Festival Film Arts Festival of Independent Cinema

FAIRS & SPECIAL EVENTS

San Francisco takes advantage of any reason to celebrate, and does its celebrating with enthusiasm and style.

January/February

Chinese New Year is celebrated in Chinatown in late January or early February with lion dances, firecrackers, and a big parade.

March

San Francisco hosts a vibrant St. Patrick's Day Parade on March 17th for its strong Irish community.

April

Japantown hosts the Cherry Blossom Festival in late April, featuring Japanese cultural events such as tea ceremonies, taiko drumming and martial arts showcases.

May

In an event unique to San Francisco, on the third Sunday in May over

100,000 joggers converge for the Bay to Breakers run, a seven-mile, cross-city mini-marathon. Many jog in outlandish costumes or naked.

Also in May, over Memorial Day weekend, the Mission District hosts Carnival festivities, including a parade, and the Latino community celebrates Cinco de Mayo on May 5.

June/July

Gay Pride Week is held in June, as is the San Francisco Lesbian/Gay/Bisexual/Transgender Pride Celebration Parade, held on the last Sunday in June. The partying starts the day before with the Dyke March and the Pink Saturday party on Castro St.

There's also a Cable Car Bell-Ringing Championship in late June or early July.

October

Halloween is perhaps San Francisco's biggest night out, with thousands of revellers heading to the Castro for the annual street party. The next two nights, November 1 and 2, the Mission District comes to life for Day of the Dead festivities.

STREET FAIRS

Street fairs are also done to the max in San Francisco. One of the most popular is the Fillmore St. Jazz Festival, held early July. The North Beach Jazz Festival is held in July or August The most renowned, however, is the Folsom Street Fair in August, which attracts all genders, expressing—and sometimes demonstrating—their sexuality and preferences. The Castro Street Fair is held in September, while Haight St. has its fair in June.

MUSIC FESTIVALS

The Stern Grove Midsummer Music Festival runs June to August in a pretty park, while the San Francisco Jazz Festival holds court from October to November. Over Labor Day weekend (beginning of September), Golden Gate Park hosts 'A la Carte, A la Park', which brings live music by top stars. Also popular in October is the San Francisco Comedy Day.

WALKING TOURS

Filled with distinct neighbourhoods, each with a distinct culture and history, San Francisco makes for the ideal city for walking tours. A number of companies run walking tours, each with its own twist. One

Rincon Park

161

reminder: many neighbourhoods are on the city's famously steep hills, so it's best to wear very comfortable shoes.

City Guides Main Library 100 Larkin St., (415) 557-4266, www.sfcityguides.org. This company offers the most comprehensive set of options, covering just about every neighbourhood in San Francisco. They also have a number of themed tours, including mural tours and ghost walks. **Map p. 76, 4B**

San Francisco City Hikes (510) 601-9207, www.cityhikes.com. This Oakland-based company also has a diverse collection of public hikes available throughout San Francisco.

Local Tastes of the City Tours 2179 12th Ave., (415) 665-0480, 888-358-TOUR, www.localtastesofthecitytours.com. This tour explores different neighbourhoods with a focus on the cuisines of each area. **Off map**

All About Chinatown Walking Tours (415) 982-8839, www.allabout chinatown.com. Offers comprehensive tours, covering historical and architectural aspects, and cultural and culinary delights. It also includes a 10-course dim sum lunch. **Map p. 8, 1-2A**

Chinatown Adventure Tours with The 'Wok Wiz' 654 Commercial St., (650) 355-9657, www.wokwiz.com. The Wok Wiz offers cultural and historical walking tours as well as cooking demonstrations. **Map p. 8, 2A**

Cruisin' the Castro from a Historical Perspective 375 Lexington St. (415) 550-8110 www.webcastro.com/castrotour. Tours of the famous neighbourhood from May through November. **Map p. 52,3C**

Haight Ashbury Flower Power Walking Tour (415) 863-1621, www.hippy gourmet.com. The tour covers 12 blocks of what might be San Francisco's most renowned neighbourhood and the heart of the hippy movement. **Map p. 100, 3-4B**

GoCar Tours (415) 474-9855. These three-wheeled, two-person, computer-guided talking cars can be driven all over San Francisco. The GPS system has presets for recorded information about specific sites. They can be picked up at Fisherman's Wharf and rented by the hour.

SPORT

SBC Park Third St. and King St. (888) 464-2468 for tickets and (800) 544-2687 for tours. Opened in 2000 as a new home for the San Francisco Giants baseball team, SBC Park (originally Pac Bell Park) was built as an old-time, small stadium in China Basin, on the east

side of the city. The views from the stands overlooking the bay are worth the visit. Boats sit offshore during the games, waiting to retrieve any home-run balls lofted into the water. There is a hole in the right-field fence purposely built to allow fans a free peek at the game. Tours of the park are available.

There are dedicated surfers who risk the bitingly cold waters and dangerous undertows of the Bay to ride the waves; you can see them often off Fort Point (see p. 142) by the Golden Gate Bridge or at Ocean Beach. This is not for amateurs, though. In fact, in spite of the fact that San Francisco is surrounded by water, locals don't spend too much time in the water; San Francisco is far from a tropical paradise. Nude bathing is allowed in certain places, though, including the Lands End beach in Lincoln Park.

163

planning

WHEN TO GO
HOW TO GET AROUND
PRACTICALITIES
FOOD AND DRINK
PLACES TO STAY

WHEN TO GO
Yes, it's California, but San Francisco in July and August can be downright chilly, thanks to intermittent fog—so dress for cool weather. April/May and September/October see the best weather of the year. Winters—December to March—are rainy. Average temperatures are highest in September, with surprisingly moderate highs of 23°C (73°F) and lows of 13°C (56°F). It's coldest in January, with highs of 14°C (57 F) and lows of 7°C (44°F).

PASSPORTS AND FORMALITIES
Visitors to the US must have a passport and, in most cases, a visa. Visitors from Canada generally do not need visas for less than 90 days. Citizens of Australia, New Zealand, Japan and many European countries may be able to visit visa-free for 90 days or less under the Visa Waiver programme. However, you must possess a machine-readable passport.

GETTING THERE
BY AIR

San Francisco International Airport (SFO) lies 13 miles south of San Francisco, along Highway 101. Airport information: (650) 821-8211.

Two smaller airports in the Bay Area also serve U.S. and Mexican destinations:
Oakland International Airport (OAK), www.oaklandairport.com, (510) 563-3300
San Jose International Airport (SJC), www.sjc.org, (408) 277-4759

MAJOR AIRLINE PHONE NUMBERS
America West (800) 2FLYAWA
American (800) AA1-CALL
Continental (800) 523-3273

Delta (800) 221-1212
Mexicana (800) 531-7921
United (800) 241-6522

BUDGET AIRLINE PHONE NUMBERS
AirTran (800) 247-8726
America West (800) 235-9292
ATA (800) 225-2995
Frontier (800) 432-1359
Midwest (800) 452-2022
JetBlue (800) 538-2583 (serves Oakland, San Jose)
Southwest (800) 435-9792 (serves Oakland, San Jose)
Ted (800) 225-5833

BY TRAIN
Long-distance train travel to San Francisco is relatively inconvenient.
Amtrak, the national rail service, stops in Emeryville (in the East Bay),
where passengers board a free shuttle bus to San Francisco's Ferry
Building. Other trains stop at Jack London Square in Oakland and are
connected by shuttle service to the Transbay Terminal at 425 Mission St.
(between First and Fremont) in San Francisco. Call (800) 872-7245 or see
www.amtrak.com for information.

BY COACH
Greyhound, the only national coach line, serves the Transbay Terminal at
425 Mission Street. For fares and schedules, call (800) 229-9424 or log
onto www.greyhound.com. Greyhound's station at the Transbay Terminal
can be reached at (415) 495-1569.

BY CAR
San Francisco can be reached from the east by US Highway 80 and from
the north or south by US 101. But if you've got time, the scenic route—
Highway 1 along the California coast—is the only way to go. It's considered
one of the most beautiful drives in the country.

GETTING TO THE CITY CENTRE
FROM THE SAN FRANCISCO AIRPORT
For more information, call San Francisco Airport's Ground
Transportation at (800) 736-2008 or check online at www.flysfo.com.

TAXIS & SHUTTLES

Taxi fare to downtown San Francisco is about $37 (for Fisherman's Wharf expect about $44). If you are headed away to an address 15 miles away from the city limits or 15 miles from the airport you will be charged 150% of the amount on the meter. Up to five people can share a taxi.

Airport shuttles can take you from the airport to the San Francisco address of your choice for $14–$17.

American Airporter Shuttle (800) 282-7758

Airport Express (415) 775-5121

Lorrie's Airporter (415) 334-9000

SuperShuttle (800) 258-3826

PUBLIC TRANSPORTATION

BART (Bay Area Rapid Transit) trains leave directly from the airport. Use the free AirTrain to get to the BART station at the International Terminal (Boarding Area G, Level 3). BART will take you to San Francisco (a one-way trip downtown is $4.95), south to Millbrae ($1.50) or to the East Bay.

BY CAR

Take US 101 north from the airport and get off at the 7th St. or 4th St. exit to reach downtown.

GETTING AROUND

The city of San Francisco is seven miles by seven miles. Many sites of interest are concentrated in the northeast, but even dedicated walkers will want to take advantage of public transport to get around.

MUNI TRANSPORT

The MUNI transport system operates buses, streetcars, metros and cable cars throughout San Francisco. The network is complex, so a MUNI map ($2.95, available at bookstores and drugstores) is a good investment.

The fare for buses, streetcars and metros is $1.25/35¢. When you pay, pick up a transfer. This slip of paper entitles you to two more bus, streetcar or metro rides during the next 90 minutes.

For unlimited rides, you can purchase a **Passport Pass** (one-day pass $9, three-day pass $15, seven-day pass $20). These passes can

The Ferry Building

be used not only on buses, streetcars and the metro, but also on cable cars. The Passport Pass can be purchased at the San Francisco Visitors Information Center (see p. 171), as well as at the MUNI kiosk upstairs from the Information Center. (415) 673-MUNI, www.sfmuni.org

BUSES
The bus system goes practically everywhere in the city, but getting all the way across town can be slow—look for limited or express buses to speed the journey. Buses commonly run from 5.30 am–12.30 am, Mon–Fri; 6 am–12.30 am, Sat; and 7.30 am–12.30 am, Sun. There is also limited 'owl service' on a few routes from 1 am–5 am each day.

METRO
On the MUNI metro lines, streetcars travel beneath Market Street and resurface as they head toward western parts of the city. The F-line uses historic streetcars from around America on the stretch from Castro Street down Market Street and to Fisherman's Wharf. It's a route many visitors will want to take advantage of.

CABLE CARS
Tickets ($3) can be bought from vending machines or from the conductor. Fare for cable cars is $3, payable to the conductor (transfers are not accepted). There can be long queues to board, especially in the summer tourist season and particularly on the lines running between Powell St. and Fisherman's Wharf. The California line (on California Street, running between Market and Van Ness) is less crowded.

BART
BART—the Bay Area Rapid Transit rail network—links San Francisco with communities in the East Bay. It also connects to the San Francisco Airport. BART starts running at 4 am weekdays, 6 am on Sat and 8 am on Sun and holidays, and continues until midnight or later. Fares are based on the distance of your travel and start at $1.25. Tickets can be purchased at any station. (415) 989-BART, www.bart.gov. For a BART map, see p. 192.

TAXIS & FERRIES
Taxis are often thin on the ground, so you may have to call for one. Taxis charge $2.85 to start, then 45 cents for each one-fifth of a mile.

Ferries run from San Francisco (the Ferry Building and/or Pier 41) to the East Bay (Oakland), Marin County (Sausalito, Tiburon), Alcatraz and Angel Island. Schedules can be found at www.baycrossings.com.

BY CAR

Driving in San Francisco can be tricky. Even if you can handle the traffic and roller coaster hills, you've still got the challenge of finding a parking place. Finding street parking is not easy, but if you do, a word of caution. when parking on a slope, turn the wheels toward the kerb (if your car is pointed downhill) or away from the kerb (if your car is pointed uphill). This is to prevent roll-aways.

The city's biggest parking garage, strategically located and relatively reasonably priced ($2 for the first hour), is at Fifth and Mission. (It's right off the Bay Bridge/Highway 80 as you come into the city. Get off at the Fifth Street exit and drive north, then turn right at Mission St.) The even more central Union Square garage is on Geary St. (between Stockton and Powell). For parking in Chinatown, try the Portsmouth Square Garage, at 733 Kearny St. (between Clay and Washington). Comprehensive parking info can be found at www.sfgov.org.

EMERGENCIES & PERSONAL SECURITY

Call **911** for all emergencies (police, fire, ambulance).
San Francisco Police Department (non-emergency calls): (415) 553-0123

HEALTH AND INSURANCE

Even emergency treatment is not free to the uninsured. Take out travellers' insurance before the trip—then, if you need treatment, call your emergency phone number to be referred to a nearby participating hospital.

HOSPITALS

San Francisco General Hospital 1001 Potrero Ave. (at 23rd), (415) 206-8000. 24-hour emergency room: (415) 206-8111. **Off map**

St. Mary's Medical Center 450 Stanyan St. (between Fulton and Hayes), (415) 668-1000. St. Mary's will see patients with non-life-threatening conditions within 30 minutes of arrival. **Map p. 127, 4D**

LATE-NIGHT PHARMACIES

The Walgreens drugstore at 498 Castro St. (at 18th) is open 24 hours a day. **Map p. 52, 1B**

A more central Walgreens, at 135 Powell St. (at O'Farrell), is open 8 am–9 pm, Mon–Fri; 9 am–5 pm, Sat. **Map p. 8, 2B**

LOST AND FOUND

San Francisco Airport (650) 821-7014

BART (510) 464-7090

Caltrain (415) 546-4482

MUNI (415) 923-6168

Police Department Property Control (415) 553-1377

Lost or stolen credit cards:

American Express (800) 554-AMEX

Mastercard (800) MC-ASSIST

Visa (800) 847-2911

CONSULATES

United Kingdom 1 Sansome St. (at Market), Suite 850, (415) 617-1300. Open 8.30 am–5 pm, Mon–Fri. Consular services 9 am–1 pm, 2–4 pm. **Map p. 8, 3B**

Australia 625 Market St., Suite 200 (at New Montgomery), (415) 536-1970. Open 8.45 am–1 pm, 2 pm–4.45 pm, Mon–Fri. **Map p. 8, 2-3B**

Irish Republic 100 Pine Street, 33rd floor. (415) 392-4214. Open 10 am–12 noon, 2–3.30 pm, Mon–Fri. **Map p. 8, 3A**

New Zealand 1 Maritime Plaza, (415) 399-1255. **Map p. 8, 3A**

DISABLED TRAVELLERS

San Francisco is well-equipped for the disabled. Virtually all of the city's buses are accessible, with lifts to board wheelchair-bound passengers and 'kneelers' that lower the bus steps for easier boarding. Light-rail vehicles use either raised platforms or lifts, depending on the station. (Cable cars are not wheelchair-accessible.) For more information on transit access, call SF Muni's Accessible Services Program at (415) 923-6142, TTY (415) 351-3443. Those who are unable to use city transit independently should look into the Paratransit taxi service (www.sfparatransit.com).

Steep inclines in some parts of town may present difficulties. The San Francisco Bike Map Walking Guide sold by the San Francisco Visitors Information Center (see p. 171), identifies hilly areas and street grades.

Access San Francisco, available on the Web at http://onlysf.sfvisitor.org/
media/downloads/accessguide2004.pdf, is an excellent resource for
many FAQs, from the locations of wheelchair-accessible pay toilets to
where to rent a car with hand controls. It's also a mini-guide that details
the level of access available at attractions, restaurants, hotels and
shopping (as well as services for the deaf and the blind).

USEFUL THINGS TO KNOW
INFORMATION OFFICES AND PUBLICATIONS

San Francisco Visitor Information Center 900 Market Street (at
Powell, downstairs in the plaza), (415) 391-2000 to order an
information packet, (415) 391-2001 for the information and events
hotline, www.sfvisitor.org. Open 9 am–5 pm, Mon–Fri; 9 am–3 pm Sat,
Sun. **Map p. 8, 2B**

The city's main paper, the *San Francisco Chronicle* (www.sfgate.com),
has extensive arts coverage, but its news reporting is widely seen as a
disappointment. The only other daily, the San Francisco Examiner
(www.sfexaminer.com), is a free tabloid with condensed coverage.

The two major free weeklies are *SF Weekly* (www.sfweekly.com) and
the *Bay Area Guardian* (www.sfbg.com). A typical issue of either
combines a few political or cultural feature stories with entertainment,
restaurant and bar reviews and listings.

MUSEUM AND DISCOUNT CARDS

CityPass ($40 for adults, $31 for children ages 5 to 17) gets you one-
time admission to the SF Museum of Modern Art, the Exploratorium,
the Asian Art Museum and your choice of either the Legion of Honor
or the California Academy of Sciences/Steinhart Aquarium. You also
get a Bay cruise with Blue & Gold Fleet, plus seven days of unlimited
rides on the city's cable cars and the rest of the MUNI transport
network. The attractions must be visited within nine days. If you do
manage to visit all of them with CityPass, you can save about 50%.
CityPass is sold online (www.citypass.com) and at participating
attractions.

Several museums (such as the Asian Art Museum and the Museum
of Modern Art) offer free admission on the first Tuesday of each
month. The Palace of the Legion of Honor offers free admission every
Tuesday. (See individual museum listings to learn about other free
admission days.)

MONEY

The most convenient, and cheapest, way to get dollars is to withdraw the money in your home bank account from an ATM (automated teller machine). Before leaving home, check with your bank to see which ATM network it is associated with. Bring your PIN (personal identification number). There is a small surcharge for using another bank's ATM.

Credit cards can also be used at ATMs to withdraw cash advances. The most prevalent networks are Cirrus (affiliated with MasterCard) and PLUS (affiliated with Visa). Credit cards are accepted at many restaurants, shops and other establishments, typically for purchases of more than $10.

Exchanging foreign currency does not typically give as good a rate as withdrawing money from an ATM. If you do exchange currency, banks generally give a better rate and/or lower commission fees than exchange offices do (inquire about rates before your transaction). Bank of America, for instance, has a branch office at 1 Powell St. (at Market., **Map p. 8, 2B**)

SALES TAX

Sales tax in San Francisco is 8.5%, added on top of the purchase price you see displayed. This is not equivalent to VAT in Europe, and there are no rebates.

TELEPHONE AND POSTAL SERVICES

Local calls from a pay phone cost 50¢, and phones are coin-operated. For long-distance or international calls, a prepaid phone card (sold in convenience stores, drugstores and elsewhere) offers significant discounts. (These work from any phone.) Making phone calls from a hotel room can be hazardous to your financial health.

Cellular phones work on the GSM network at 1900MHz. A tri-band GSM phone will work in the US but a dual-band GSM 900/1800 MHz standard phone will not.

The **country code for the United States is 1**. The **area code for San Francisco and Marin County is 415**. The East Bay (Alameda and Contra Costa counties, including Oakland and Berkeley) is in the 510 area code. San Mateo County (the Peninsula, south of San Francisco) has the 650 area code.

For **directory assistance**, call 411 (for numbers within the local area code). For help in placing a call, dial 0 for the operator, but be aware that operator-assisted calls cost more.

Dialling the UK from the US (011-44) + number without the initial zero

Dialling the US from the UK (00-1) + number

AT&T (800) 225-5288

MCI (800) 888-8000

Sprint (800) 366-2255

POSTAL SERVICES

Stamps are available at post offices and some supermarkets. Deliveries within the United States are 23¢ (postcards) or 37¢ (letters less than one ounce). Sending a postcard overseas costs 70¢; sending a letter overseas costs 80¢.

INTERNET CENTERS

Anyone can log on for 15 minutes, free, at any branch of the **San Francisco Public Library**. The library's main branch is at 100 Larkin St. (at Grove), (415) 557-4400, **Map p. 76, 4B**. For a complete list of branch locations, check http://sfpl.lib.ca.us/.

Kinko's has several locations in the city and is open late. You can buy time on their computers for Internet access and/or word processing. The Nob Hill location is open 24 hours a day; it's at 1800 Van Ness Ave., (415) 292-2500. **Off map**

A large and central place is **Cafe.com**, 970 Market St. (between Fifth and Sixth), (415) 433-4001. Open 9 am–9 pm. **Map p. 8, 1C**

Brainwash, at 1122 Folsom Street, is a laundromat/internet cafe. Open 7 am–11 pm daily. **Map p. 8, 1-2D**

San Francisco leads the country in wireless Internet access. Hundreds of cafés, restaurants, and hotels in the city offer Wi-Fi access. Even Union Square has a free Wi-Fi centre. All you need is a laptop capable of receiving the wireless signal.

WEB RESOURCES

TOURISM
Visitor Information Center www.sfvisitor.org

The San Francisco Chronicle's excellent **Bay Area Traveler** www.sfgate.com/traveler

TRANSPORT
www.511.org

HISTORY
A **virtual museum** of San Francisco www.sfmuseum.org

FUN
Webcams of the Golden Gate Bridge, the Transamerica Pyramid and other places www.sfgate.com/liveviews

OPENING TIMES
MUSEUMS
Opening times for museums vary considerably. Most museums will be open between 10 am and 5 pm, and most will be closed on Mon. But check the individual museum to be sure (and even then, allow for slight variations, depending on the season). Some museums stop letting visitors in shortly before closing time.

SHOPS
Shops tend to be open roughly 10 am–7 pm, Mon–Sat, and 11 am–6 pm, Sun. Boutique stores, or stores in less-trafficked areas, might close an hour earlier (or be closed on Sunday). Department stores might be open an hour or so later.

PUBLIC HOLIDAYS
January 1	New Year's Day
January, 3rd Mon	Martin Luther King Jr Day
February, 3rd Mon	Presidents' Day
May, last Mon	Memorial Day
July 4	Independence Day
September, 1st Mon	Labor Day
October, 2nd Mon	Columbus Day
November 11	Veterans; Day
November, 4th Thur	Thanksgiving
December 25	Christmas Day

TIME
San Francisco is in the Pacific Standard Time (PST) zone, GMT/UTC -8. Daylight saving begins for most of the US at 2 am on the first Sun of April and ends at 2 am on the last Sun of October.

TIPPING
Give 15% in a restaurant or bar when your food or drink is brought to you. Tips in a restaurant or bar are typically left on the table. Taxi drivers

and hairdressers should also get 15%. At the hotel or airport, give
bellboys and porters $1-$2 per bag.

WEIGHTS AND MEASURES
The United States uses traditional English (Imperial) units of
measurement (but many goods, like packaged foods, are labelled in both
traditional and metric units). Clothing and shoe sizes also differ from UK
and European sizes.

PLACES TO STAY
The city's hotels are heavily concentrated in the downtown area and
thinly scattered elsewhere. The selection below is biased in favour of
smaller properties that have personality and offer value for money.
Prices are typically per room and vary according to season and location.
It's best to make reservations well in advance, especially in the summer.
The San Francisco Convention and Visitors Bureau has a hotel
reservation service (call (888) 782-9673 or check www.sfvisitor.org).

PRICE GUIDE
$ up to $90 for a double room
$$$ $90–$140
$$$$ $140–$190
$$$$$ $190 and above

GOLDEN GATE PARK
$$ **The Red Victorian** 1655 Haight St. (at Cole), (415) 864-1978,
     www.redvic.com. A peace-and-love ethos prevails at this
     Victorian home in Haight-Ashbury near the park; each room is
     done in its own far-out theme. **Map p. 100, 3B**

PRESIDIO
$$ **Seal Rock 545** Point Lobos Ave. (at 48th), (415) 752-8000, (888)
     SEAL-ROCK, www.sealrockinn.com. At this budget hotel near
     Lincoln Park, most rooms look onto the ocean, and many
     contain fireplaces. **Map p. 126, 1C**

$$$ **Laurel Inn** 444 Presidio Ave. (at California), (415) 567-8467, (800) 552-8735, www.thelaurelinn.com. Contemporary yet warm; the Laurel Inn is in Pacific Heights. **Off map**

THE MISSION/CASTRO

$$ **The Inn San Francisco** 943 South Van Ness Ave. (between 20th & 21st), (415) 641-0188, (800) 359-0913, www.InnSF.com. Elegant, with ornate, old-fashioned furniture. **Map p. 52, 4B**

CIVIC CENTER TO MARINA

$ **Marina Inn** 3110 Octavia St. (at Lombard), (415) 928-1000, (800) 274-1420, www.marinainn.com. This cosy Victorian house is close to the yacht harbour. **Off map**

$$ **Argonaut Hotel** 495 Jefferson St. (at Hyde), (866) 415-0704, (415) 563-0800, www.argonauthotel.com. This immensely popular hotel, located at the end of Fisherman's Wharf, features relatively large rooms with nautical themes. **Map p. 39, 1A**

Chateau Tivoli 1057 Steiner St. (at Golden Gate), (800) 228-1647, www.chateautivoli.com. This restored Victorian house is a bed-and-breakfast whose fine furnishings come from the estates of the Vanderbilts and Charles de Gaulle. **Map p. 76, 1B**

Edward II Inn & Suites 3155 Scott St. (between Lombard and Greenwich), (415) 922-3000, www.edwardii.com. Tricked out with canopy beds and other similar items, the homey Edward II offers 32 rooms and seven suites. **Off map**

$$$ **Archbishop's Mansion** 1000 Fulton St. (at Steiner), (415) 563- 7872, (800) 543-5820, www.jdvhospitality.com/hotels/hotel/2. This century-old building in the style of a French chateau, near postcard-esque Alamo Square, features an opera theme in each room. **Map p. 76, 1B**

$$$$ **Drisco** 2901 Pacific Ave. (at Broderick), (415) 346-2880, (800) 634-7277, www.hoteldrisco.com. Classical elegance amidst the mansions of Pacific Heights, with views of downtown and the Bay. **Off map**

DOWNTOWN

$ **Nob Hill Motor Inn** 1630 Pacific Ave. (at Polk), (415) 775-8160, (800) 343-6900, www.staysf.com/nobhill. This moderately priced motel offers good-sized rooms and free parking, not far from Fisherman's Wharf. **Off map**

San Remo 2237 Mason St. (at Chestnut), (415) 776-8688, (800) 352-REMO, www.sanremohotel.com. This bargain pension's rooms have antique furniture and memorabilia; baths are shared. **Map p. 39, 2B**

$$$ **Orchard Hotel** 665 Bush St. (between Powell and Stockton), (415) 362-8878, (888) 717-2881, www.theorchardhotel.com. A boutique hotel close to Union Square done in warm colours and furnished in Balinese wood. **Map p. 8, 2B**

Hotel Adagio 550 Geary St. (between Taylor and Jones), (415) 775-5000, (800) 228-8830, www.thehoteladagio.com. The smart-looking Adagio boasts largish rooms in earth tones. **Map p. 8, 1B**

White Swan Inn 845 Bush St. (between Taylor and Mason), (415) 775-1755, (800) 999-9570, fax (415) 775-5717, www.jdvhospitality.com/hotels/hotel/16. This bed-and-breakfast seems to define cosy, with a fireplace in each room and a 'ye olde' style of furniture. **Map p. 8, 1B**

$$$$ **Campton Place Hotel** 340 Stockton St. (at Sutter), (415) 781-5555, www.camptonplace.com. A luxury property well-known for impeccable service and lavish interiors. **Map p. 8, 2B**

W Hotel 181 3d St. (at Howard), (415) 777-5300. www.whotels.com. One of the city's most stylish, with pampering amenities; most rooms look onto the Bay Bridge. **Map p. 8, 3B**

Pan Pacific San Francisco 500 Post St. (at Mason), (415) 771-8600, http://sanfrancisco.panpacific.com. A Union Square property with marble bathrooms and other charming design touches. **Map p. 8, 1B**

Mandarin Oriental 222 Sansome St. (between Pine and California), (415) 276-9888, www.mandarinoriental.com. Gorgeous panoramas of the city crown the guest experience inside this posh hotel. **Map p. 8, 3B**

HOSTELS Hostelling International runs four hostels in the San Francisco area (near Civic Center, Downtown, Fisherman's Wharf and in Marin, across the Golden Gate Bridge), which offer a few private rooms (roughly $70) as well as beds in dorm-style rooms (roughly $26). A credit card is required for advance booking; book well ahead for summer, as demand is high. See www.norcalhostels.org.

art glossary

Abstract Expressionism A term applied to the work of a group of artists active in the 1940s–1960s who shared the same philosophical approach to art, if not the same style or technique. Jackson Pollock, Mark Rothko, Willem de Kooning and others were concerned with the attempt to translate emotion to the canvas. Originally called the 'New York School', the term Abstract Expressionism was coined in 1936 by Richard Coates of the *New Yorker* magazine. By the 1950s it had become the dominant artistic movement in the US.

Adams, Ansel (1902–1984) Acclaimed San-Francisco-born photographer, known for both his striking nature photography and for his activism and dedication to protecting wilderness spaces. Adams was instrumental in founding two photography groups, Group f/64 in 1932, and Friends of Photography in 1967. He fought for recognition of photography as an art form and favoured an artistic philosophy that rejected painterly techniques or manipulation. At the time of his death, Adams' photographs had appeared in over 500 exhibitions and set auction records.

Applegarth, George (1875–1972) Architect and Bay Area native, Applegarth studied drawing with Bernard Maybeck, and architecture at the École des Beaux-Arts in Paris. Applegarth is best known for designing the Palace of the Legion of Honor (1924), commissioned by Alma Spreckels, and the Spreckles Mansion at 2080 Washington Ave., now home to novelist Danielle Steel.

Aulenti, Gae (b. 1927) Italian designer and architect responsible for transforming the former San Francisco Main Library into the Asian Art Museum. Aulenti's other museum projects include the Museé d'Orsay in Paris, the Palazzo Grassi in Venice and the Contemporary Art Gallery at Centre Pompidou in Paris.

Bender, Albert (1866–1941) Insurance executive and patron of the arts, Bender was instrumental in bringing Diego Rivera to San Francisco to work on the San Francisco Arts Institute mural commission. Frida Kahlo gave her painting *Frida and Diego Rivera* (1931) to Bender in thanks; Bender donated this, Rivera's *Flower*

Carriers (1935) and 34 other paintings to the San Francisco Museum of Modern Art to start their collection (see p. 9). He is also known as a patron of Ansel Adams, as well as other photographers, and financed Adams' first portfolio in 1926.

Bliss, Walter (1873–1956) and William Faville (1866–1946) Architects known for the St. Francis Hotel, the Geary Theatre, the Metropolitan Club and the California State Building. Bliss and Faville favoured conservative designs and received a number of bank commissions, including the Bank of California and the Bank of America Building on Halladie Plaza.

Botta, Mario (born 1943) Swiss Modernist architect, Botta originally worked as an assistant to Le Corbusier and Louis I. Kahn. He is known for his design of a Capuchin convent in Lugano and the Balerna Craft Centre, as well as the San Francisco Museum of Modern Art, completed in 1995 (see p. 9).

Brown, Arthur Page (1859–96) Architect best known for designing the San Francisco Ferry Building (see p. 22), as well as Trinity Church and the Crocker Building. Brown died during construction of the Ferry Building, after being injured in a horse and buggy accident.

Brown, Arthur Jr. (1874–1957) Architect known for his collaboration on a series of significant San Francisco landmarks, including City Hall (see p. 90), the War Memorial Opera House and Veterans Building (see p. 135), Coit Tower (see p. 20), Temple Emanu-El, and the San Francisco-Oakland Bay Bridge.

Brundage, Avery (1887–1975) Chicago industrialist and collector Brundage was also an athlete; he competed in the 1912 Olympics and was president of the International Olympic Committee for twenty years. In appreciation for Brundage's support of the Japanese Olympic bid in 1964, the Japanese government deregulated several protected art objects, which allowed Brundage to purchase them. In 1966 Brundage donated his art collection to the City of San Francisco, with the stipulation that a building be constructed to house it. His collection still makes up a large portion of the Asian Art Museum's permanent collection (see p. 77).

Bufano, Beniamino 'Benny' (1898–1970) Sculptor and muralist known for simplified forms and rounded smooth figures. His work can be seen throughout the Bay Area. A radical, Bufano was fired from his teaching position at the San Francisco Institute of Art in 1923. In an unusual act of protest against World War I, he severed his finger and sent it to President Woodrow Wilson. Bufano's steel-and-granite sculpture Sun Yat-sen (1937) can be found in Chinatown (see p. 24), in St. Mary's Square at 651 California St.

City Beautiful Movement Begun in the late 19th C, the City Beautiful movement called for improving the American urban environment in order to bring American cities into parity with cities of Europe. This was to be done through the creation of Beaux-Arts urban centres. San Francisco owes Civic Center (see p. 79) to the movement, and to the leadership of Mayor James Rolph. Civic Center now includes City Hall (1916); the old library building, now the Asian Art Museum (1917; see p. 77); the Civic Auditorium (1915); the California State Building (1922); the Opera House (1931); and the Veteran's War Memorial Building (1931). Recent additions include Lousie M. Davies Symphony Hall (1981), the new State of California Building (1986) and the new Main Library building (1996).

Cubism A style pioneered by Pablo Picasso and Georges Braque between 1908 and 1912. Cubism attempted to convey the essence of a three-dimensional object by painting it from multiple perspectives simultaneously. Picasso and Braque were influenced by the work of Paul Cezanne and by tribal art, though Braque would come to deny the latter.

Diebenkorn, Richard (1922–93) Berkeley painter best known for his abstract aerial landscapes, the *Ocean Park* series, which he began in 1967. The series is named after the suburban community in Santa Monica where Diebenkorn lived while teaching at the University of Californion, Los Angeles.

Fauvism Named after the wild beasts (*fauves*) that one reviewer claimed must have painted Matisse's *Femme au Chapeau* (1905). Fauvism was a less naturalistic style, known for shocking colours, and Fauvist painters include Henri Matisse, Andre Derain and Albert Marquet.

Friends of Photography A photography organisation founded in 1967 by Ansel Adams, Morley Baer, Beaumont and Nancy Newhall, and Brett Weston, among others. The Friends worked to promote photography by holding exhibits and workshops, publishing catalogues and establishing awards for emerging photographers. The Friends of Photography disbanded in 2001, having donated their 3,000-volume library to the San Francisco Art Institute.

Group f/64 West Coast photography group founded in 1932 by Ansel Adams, Edward Weston, Willard Van Dyke, Imogen Cunningham. The name refers to the small lens aperture used to increase sharpness. Members of Group f/64 sought to have photography recognised as a fine art and promoted a 'straight approach' to photography that eschewed painterly techniques and the manipulation of the image.

Haas, Elise Stern (1893–1990) Arts patron and philanthropist, Haas was the daughter of Levi Strauss & Co. president Sigmund Stern. An active supporter of the Museum of Modern Art (see p. 9), Hass served as chair of the board from 1964–1966. On her death in 1990, she donated her art collection—including Matisse's seminal work *Femme au Chapeau* (1905)—to the museum.

Hamlin, Edith (1902–1992) California Modernist painter Hamlin's murals can be seen at Coit Tower (see p. 20) and Mission High School. She also painted murals in Chicago, Los Angeles, and at the Department of the Interior in Washington DC. A prolific painter, she was also known for her landscapes.

Herzog, Jacques (b. 1950) and Pierre de Meuron (b. 1950). Pritzker-winning Swiss architects known for transforming the Bankside Power Station in London into the Tate Modern Museum. In San Francisco. Their copper-cloaked design has been selected for the new de Young Museum, which will be the largest copper building ever built.

Howard, John Galen (1864–1931) Architect and founder of the architecture department at the University of California at Berkeley. Howard worked with Frederick Meyer and John Reid, Jr. to plan the San Francisco Civic Center and the Bill Graham Auditorium, on the south side of Civic Center Plaza.

Howard, Robert B. (1896–1983) Sculptor and painter, Howard was the oldest son of architect John Galen Howard. His early work is included in the Coit Tower murals (see p. 20), as well as at the Pacific Stock Exchange Luncheon Club (now City Club). Howard's large block sculpture of killer whales is displayed at the Academy of Sciences in Golden Gate Park (see p. 111).

Kelham, George (1871–1936) Architect, educated at Harvard and the École des Beaux-Arts in Paris, Kelham designed the Main Library building (now the Asian Art Museum; see p. 77), the Federal Reserve Building and the Russ Building. Kelham served as university architect for the University of California at Berkeley from 1927 to1938.

Labaudt, Lucien (1880–1943) French-born Labaudt came to San Francisco in 1910 and worked as a costume designer and muralist. He is best known for the Beach Chalet murals, located at the west side of Golden Gate Park, but his work can also be seen at Coit Tower (see p. 20) and at George Washington High School.

Libeskind, Daniel (b. 1946) Best known for his design of the Jewish Museum in Berlin. In San Francisco, Libeskind will transform the 1917 Jessie St. substation into the new Contemporary Jewish Museum.

Maybeck, Bernard (1862–1957) Bay Area architect best known designing the Palace of Fine Arts and its Lagoon (see p. 26), built as part of the 1915 Panama-Pacific International Exposition. Maybeck's design was rebuilt in concrete in the 1960s, the only portion of the Exposition to be preserved. Maybeck was also the first Bay Area architect awarded the American Institute of Architects Gold Medal of Honour.

Meyer, Frederick Herman (1876–1961) San Francisco-born architect selected in 1911, along with John Galen Howard and John Reid, Jr. to devise a plan for the new Civic Center. Meyer was a supporter of the City Beautiful Movement and, with Howard and Reid, was responsible for selecting the beaux-arts design of Arthur Brown Jr. for San Francisco City Hall.

Mission Revival Popular around the turn of the century, the architectural style of Mission Revival featured tiled roofs, plastered walls, arched doorways and low rooflines that echoed the design of the original mission buildings constructed in the late 18th C.

Morgan, Julia (1872–1957) First woman to graduate from the University of California at Berkeley with a degree in Civil Engineering, and first woman to be admitted to the architecture department of the École des Beaux-Arts in Paris. Morgan designed over 700 buildings, many of them Arts and Crafts homes in the Bay Area. In San Francisco she is known for the Katherine Delmar Burke School, now University High School, and the Heritage Retirement Community residence, though perhaps her most famous commission is Hearst Castle at San Simeon.

Oldfield, Otis (1890–1969) A painter, Oldfield studied with Arthur Best and at the Academie Julian in Paris, before returning to California and teaching art at the California School of Fine Arts. A muralist on the Coit Tower project (see p. 20), Oldfield is known for his bold modernist style.

Olmsted, Frederick E. (1911–1972) San Francisco born painter, sculptor and architect, Olmsted collaborated on the Coit Tower murals (see p. 20) and had various other commissions around the city.

Pereira, William L. (1909–85) Architect known for designing San Francisco's iconic Transamerica Pyramid (see p. 22) in 1972.

Pflueger, Timothy (1892–1946) Modernist architect Pflueger worked on projects the Pacific Telephone Company Building, the Castro Theater (see p. 57), the Transbay Terminal, City College of San Francisco, the Pacific Stock Exchange Building, the Macy's building on Union Square, and the Union Square plaza and underground parking structure—the first of its kind.

Polk, Willis Jefferson (1867–1924) A noted architect, Polk designed numerous residences, including the Gibbs Mansion. He was also instrumental in planning the 1915 Panama-Pacific International Exhibition, acting as the initial supervising architect. His Hallidie Building is considered one of the first glass curtain-wall structures.

Rivera, Diego (1886–1957) Mexican muralist and life-long Marxist, Rivera sought to fuse his artistic and political vision. Many of his murals sparked controversy. Rivera's work in San Francisco includes murals at the Art Institute, San Francisco City College and the City Club (formerly the Pacific Stock Exchange Luncheon Club). Riviera is also known for his tempestuous marriage to painter Frida Kahlo.

Rockefeller, John, III (1906–78) Industrialist, philanthropist, and art collector, Rockefeller and his wife Blanchette donated over 100 items from their collection of American Art to the de Young museum (see p. 101), thus providing the museum with the largest collection of American Art on the West Coast.

Spreckles, Alma de Bretteville (1881–1968) The daughter of Danish immigrants, she grew up on a farm in San Francisco and worked in her family's laundry and as an artist's model before marrying Adolph Spreckels, a wealthy sugar baron. An avid art collector and philanthropist, Spreckels built the Palace of the Legion of Honor (see p. 128) to house her art collection, and donated both to the city of San Francisco. She was also instrumental in establishing a maritime museum. She modelled for the statue that tops the column in Union Square (see p. 24).

Stackpole, Ralph (1885–1973) Painter and sculptor Stackpole is known for his monumental figures, *Mother Earth* and *Man and His Inventions*, located in front of the Pacific Coast Stock Exchange (now the City Club), and for his work on the Coit Tower murals (see p. 20).

Still, Clyfford (1904–80) A Colour Field colour painter who helped pioneer the use of mural-sized canvases. Still taught at the California School of Fine Arts from 1933 to 1950. In 1975, Still donated 28 of his monumental canvases to SFMOMA (see p. 9), with the stipulation that they be displayed together in a room dedicated to his work.

Strauss, Joseph Baerman (1870–1938) Architect of the Golden Gate Bridge, Strauss fought opposition from Southern Pacific Railroad and the US War Department before getting approval for the 1.7-mile suspension bridge. Strauss died a year after the bridge was completed.

Wright, Frank Lloyd (1867–1959) Architect known for innovative and contemporary designs that meld form and function. Wright designed over 1,000 buildings in his career of 70 years; one, in San Francisco, is the Xanadu Gallery (designed as the V.C. Morris Gift Shop in 1948) on Maiden Lane.

Zakheim, Bernard Baruch (1896–1985) Polish-born muralist and sculptor Zakheim's work often depicted historical scenes of suffering or protest. Zakheim sought asylum in the US in 1920, after World War I, and studied art at the present day Art Institute. His San Francisco commissions include Coit Tower (see p. 20), the Jewish Community Center, and the murals at the University of California Medical Center (Toland Hall).

index

Page numbers in italics indicate Art Glossary references.

art/shop/eat San Francisco
First edition 2005

Published by Blue Guides Limited, a Somerset Books company
The Studio, 51 Causton Street, London SW1P 4AT

ISBN 0-905131-07-0

Published in the United States of America by
WW Norton & Company, Inc
500 Fifth Avenue, New York, NY 10110, USA

ISBN 0-393-32833-3

Editor: Maya Mirsky   Copy and map editing: Mark Griffith
Layout: Katalin Seregélyes   Volume design: Anikó Kuzmich, Regina Rácz
Series devised by Gemma Davies

Photo editors: Hadley Kincade, Róbert Szabó Benke

SOMERSET BOOKS

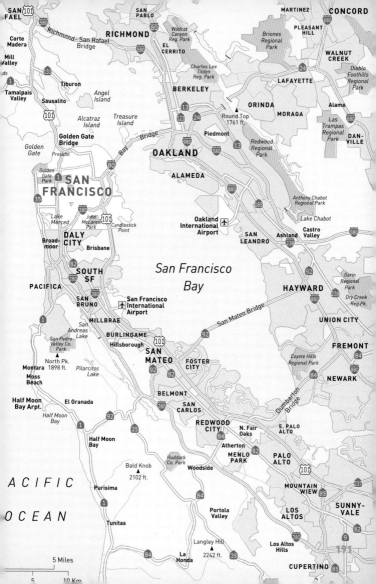

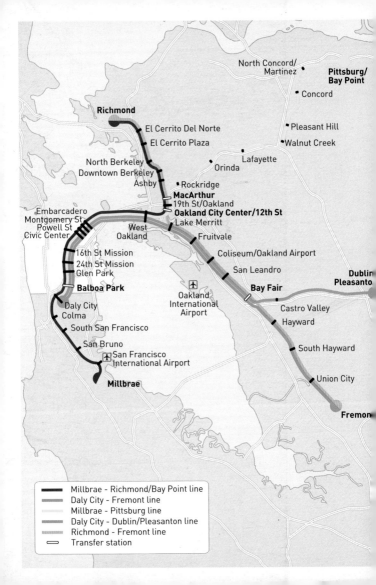